Erich Schröder

Encounters in Peru

Erich Schröder

Encounters in Peru

Experiences of a frequent traveler
in South America,
told by Erich Schröder,
dedicated with gratitude to all
persons mentioned in this book.

9 783751 997508

Bibliografische Information der Deutschen Nationalbibliothek:
Die Deutsche Nationalbibliothek verzeichnet diese
Publikation in der Deutschen Nationalbibliografie;
detaillierte bibliografische Daten sind im Internet
über http://dnb.dnb.de abrufbar.

Herstellung und Verlag:
BoD – Books on Demand, Norderstedt

ISBN: 9 783751 997508

CONTENT

PERU

OTHER DESTINATIONS IN LATIN AMERICA

REFLECTIONS ON TRAVELLING

Peru

Meeting on Machu Picchu

I had reached out my hand to help Teresa up to a high level and had not let go of her hand. Now we both climbed up this pyramid-shaped hill where friends, lovers and couples meet. We had to touch a small granite column together, which protrudes on an artfully hewn stone block. This stone, called "Intihuatana" in the Inca language Quechua, which means "the place where the sun is tied up", probably served as an astronomical instrument to define the seasons. One of the many myths around Machu Picchu promises eternal love or at least eternal friendship when they touch the tip together. Teresa knew this old legend; she had told me the story and now we were both curious to try it out. So, we entered the top of the pyramid and joined a group of couples around the stone block who had come here with the same intention. Then finally the time had come, the small granite column was within reach. I touched the stone with my left hand, my right let go of her hand and embraced her waist. Teresa put her right hand on the stone and ran her left hand over my back. She could not suppress a slight tremor of her hand. Would I kiss her now? Then she felt my lips on her forehead and held her breath. But it remained this light caress. I pulled her a little closer to me and then let go, only to take her hand again.

So, we had done it. Would this short moment be enough to bring the myth of Machu Picchu to us and make the promise come true? We only knew each other for about two hours! Teresa, a pretty 18-year-old girl, was on her first big trip with her aunt Iris. Her thick shoulder-length black hair and slim figure made her look even younger. She wore a long-sleeved white shirt, decorated with a large rose embroidery in the front, over her jeans. A light red poncho lay ready over her handbag to protect her from the cold air of the Andes.

The train from Cusco to Aguas Calientes is the only connection that brings tourists and locals from Cusco along the Rio Urobamba to the foot of the mountain of Machu Picchu. The road ends shortly after the village of Ollantaytambo, where there are also well-preserved remains of an Inca settlement. Alternatively, Machu Picchu can be reached by a three-day and quite tiring hike on the Inca Trail, which is preferred by some adventurous tourists.

In two compartments of the train sat Teresa and her aunt Iris, her father's youngest sister, and four friends of her aunt. I had been assigned a seat in the middle of this group. So next to me sat a young woman who was talking to the others in the group. Like most tourists, I looked out of the window without paying attention to the conversation in the compartment, which I did not understand too much of anyway. But my neighbor was curious, she had looked at me from time to time in a stealthy manner. I was just 30 years old at the time, wearing black jeans, a brown suede jacket and worn sports shoes and had only put a linen shopping bag in front of me. In it she spotted a camera and a book, obviously a travel guide. A tourist, she knew, a gringo as the Peruvians say, probably from the USA. Finally, she took heart and spoke to me, but I did not understand her question. So, she asked Teresa for support and translation, and Teresa sat down with us:

"Where do you come from?"
"Germany. And you?"
"I am Peruvian."
I should have guessed it.
"What are you doing in Germany?
"I am student at university, medicine.
"Students must be rich in Germany, traveling to South America?

I was not rich, had scraped together my money for the cheap flight and was now sitting on a train in the middle of South America with rather empty pockets. At that moment it seemed rather adventurous even to me. But the basis for a longer conversation for the rest of the train journey was there. The whole group asked question after question, they wanted to know everything about me, and Teresa was well occupied with the mutual translations. To the displeasure of my seat neighbor, Teresa and not her with me was now the focus of the rest of the conversation, she later complained about this to Teresa.

From the train station Aguas Calientes at the height of the Rio Urobamba, a small armada of minibuses drives the visitors over a narrow private road with numerous serpentines up to the mountain to the en-

3

trance of the Inca city Machu Picchu. Clever tourists spend the night cheaply in Aguas Calientes or expensively in an accommodation close to the entrance of Machu Picchu and get to the old Inca city before the tourist trains arrive to experience the sunrise. But this is not always successful, because the mountain is often covered by clouds. But just to experience the huge complex in its loneliness without the stream of tourists is worth every effort, even in the fog.

For Aunt Iris and her friends, it was almost like a holy duty to visit Machu Picchu once in a lifetime - but they were not particularly keen on climbing. But in Machu Picchu there are considerable ascents and endless stairs with a total of more than 3,000 steps. So, it was easy for Teresa and me to break away from the group and explore the old city together on our own. The path led us directly to the pyramid of friendship to the Intihuatana stone, where "the sun is captured".

The journey to Cusco

At that time Teresa lived with her aunt Iris in Lima, where she attended Unifé, a university for women only, to study languages. She came from Chiclayo, where her family lived. But her mother had insisted on this university.

From Chiclayo, the largest city in the northwest of Peru, Teresa commuted by bus at the beginning of each semester to the capital Lima, a 13-hour journey on the famous Panamericana Road 800 kilometers south. The Panamericana runs from Alaska in the north of the USA to Tierra del Fuego in the south of Chile with a break between Panama and Colombia, where there is no road connection. In Peru it is the only continuous north-south connection over a length of 2,500 km. For long distances, the road runs through the desert along the Pacific coast. It touches the main Peruvian cities, which have always developed like oases where a river flows from the high mountains of the Andes into the Pacific, Piura in the north, then Chiclayo, and on the way to Lima, Trujillo and Chimbote are passed. Further south, the Panamericana passes through Arequipa and, just before the border with Chile, the small border town of Tacna. The highly frequented road is the most important connection in the country for trucks of all kinds, long-distance buses, public regional transport, and private vehicles. It is often broken, which leads to construction sites and traffic jams. Especially in times of political tension, which is not uncommon in Peru, there are also numerous police and military controls on the route.

There are several companies in Peru that operate long-distance buses. Each company has its own stops and bus stations. In contrast to the often old and rickety local buses, the long-distance buses are usually in quite good condition and sufficiently comfortable. Some companies also offer first class with reclining seats and meals. On long stages without a stop, there are occasional breaks at rest stops that have contracts with the bus company. Peruvians love window seats in the bus, but not to look out. They close the curtains, put a jacket against the window and your head on it and fall asleep immediately, at the latest when the bus starts rolling.

There is also a bus service from Lima to Cusco, which is operated by several companies. It is 1.100km long and takes about 22 hours. Aunt Iris and her friends probably did not want to do this to themselves and instead allowed the small travel group to take the one-hour flight. Most flights from Lima to Cusco leave early in the morning. The few flights that leave in the afternoon are often unpunctual or cancelled. This is due to the special location of the city of Cusco, in the middle of the Andes mountains at about 3,400 m altitude between snow-covered peaks. During the day it can get quite warm in the valley basin, occasionally up to 30 degrees, but at night it is always very cold, often frosty. In the morning, the sky over Cusco is usually clear, and over the day clouds often gather, into which the peaks of the surrounding mountains plunge. In addition, the approach to Cusco leads through a long and curved valley between the mountain peaks from where the runway is reached in a narrow left turn. This approach is not easy even with good visibility, in clouds almost impossible, as even the usual radar approach aids cannot be used on this complicated flight path. The approach to Cusco is a challenge for every pilot.

I had also come to Cusco by plane and had already had an awfully long journey behind me. This trip was supposed to bring me some distraction after a divorce proceeding that had just been completed and to open up new perspectives. The flight with the then low-cost airline SATA, which I had found after some searching, was almost cancelled for me because the ordered ticket (at that time still a paper ticket) did not arrive despite several reminders. It finally arrived by express courier/night delivery the evening before my planned departure. The flight started in Zurich and had stops in the Caribbean and in Bogota, the capital of Colombia, on the way to Lima. So, I was on the road for about 16 hours from Zurich and reached Lima around 02:00 a.m. There were considerable queues in front of the entry counters, but the formalities themselves were uncomplicated. The official even spoke English, which, as I was to learn shortly afterwards, was by no means to be expected in Lima. When I happily found my black shoulder bag on the luggage belt, it was already 03:00 o'clock. So, I entered the airport hall, practically without speaking or understanding a word of Spanish, and was immediately surrounded by a horde of probably illegal taxi drivers who tried to grab my shoulder bag to catch me for their taxi. I was able to ward this off successfully and observed that they did not lead other passengers to the taxis that were waiting in a row but somewhere on the parking place behind it. After they could not land at my place and the situation had calmed down a bit, my search for an official taxi was successful and I got a ride to Plaza San Martin in the old center of Lima. In my travel guide I had read that there are many and partly cheap hotels and hostels in the surroundings of this place. There I found a simple hotel and also managed to make clear to the receptionist that I needed a room and a beer, with which I immediately learned my first Spanish phrases from him. I stayed in Lima for two more days and continued learning how to get a meal in a restaurant. But then I wanted to go on to Cusco.

The flight from Lima to Cusco is not only a challenge for the pilot but also for the passengers. Lima is located by the sea, i.e. at sea level, and a good hour later, at an altitude of 3,300 meters, the passenger receives his suitcases. This is not for everyone, and at the latest when you have carried your luggage a little bit or when the path is rising, most arriving passengers run out of air at first. If the complaints persist one speaks of the altitude sickness, the Peruvians call it "Soroche". The usual therapy there is coca leaves, which are mostly offered as tea infusion. The positive effect is not long in coming. I allowed myself a few days of acclimatization to explore the beautiful city of Cusco in peace. Then I booked the train to Machu Picchu.

Cusco - the Inca capital

"Well, did he kiss you," Aunt Iris asked curiously.
"No," Teresa replied and immediately noticed that she blushed a little. Aunt Iris had not missed this either, but she did not go into it any further. She had made herself comfortable on the bed of her shared hotel room in the center of Cusco to put her feet up a bit after the exhausting hike through Machu Picchu. Teresa was sitting at the small table of the room. For the evening I had made an appointment to visit a Pena in the city and drink Vino Caliente (hot red wine) against the cold of the night and eat some tapas. Penas are

mostly small but overcrowded pubs offering live music of Peruvian folklore as well as drinks and tapas.

Cusco is a highlight of every Peruvian trip; the city is not missing in any package tour offer. The capital of the former Inca empire was founded by the first Inca, Manco Capac, the son of the sun, according to legend. Scientists date the foundation approximately to the twelfth century. The development of the city into a political and cultural center then took place around the beginning of the 14th century. Several generations of Inca rulers subsequently ruled the rapidly expanding and powerful Inca empire from Cusco. On November 15, 1533, the Spaniard Francisco Pizarro captured the city of Cusco after having captured the last Inca ruler Atahualpa in the Battle of Cajamarca on November 16, 1532, and then killed him despite obtaining a huge ransom in gold.

Today Cusco captivates by its location in the middle of the Andes mountains and by a beautiful old town with buildings from the colonial period but also still well-preserved foundation walls from the Inca era. Some churches stand on the foundation walls of the Incas; at that time, it was probably a special concern of the Spaniards to demolish the existing non-Christian temples or also important cultural or political buildings and to build catholic churches on their foundations. A good example of this is the Iglesia de Santo Domingo, where the foundation walls from the Inca period are well preserved and easily recognizable.

The center of the city is - as in all bigger cities in Peru - the Plaza de Armas. The middle of the plaza is formed by a beautiful park with numerous benches, in the center of which is a fountain, the Monumento del Inca. Two big churches dominate the plaza, the massive cathedral at the east side and the smaller but more beautiful Iglesia de la Compania de Jesus at the south side. Around the plaza there are some hotels, several restaurants, travel agencies and souvenir shops. And the one or two Penas that, if they are open, are easy to find, already due to their noise volume.

We had arranged to meet at the Plaza de Armas at 7 p.m. I was there on time and started my walk around the square. A first round, and nothing to see of Teresa. A second round and a third. What I did not know at that time was that punctuality in Peru has a different meaning than in Germany. While we understand punctuality to mean that an agreed time is kept as closely as possible, that would be quite impolite in Peru. For example, if you are invited to a house, it would be very possible to meet the lady of the house at the agreed time, still uncombed and dressed in house clothes. Usually you should arrive about 1 hour later.

And so it happened. Around 7:45 p.m. I finally saw Teresa, aunt Iris and her friends walking across the square. After a friendly greeting we went to the next Pena, which was in a quiet side street to the Plaza de Armas. But the closer we came to the restaurant the less quiet it was. I was not promised too much in the description of the restaurant. A big bunch of people surrounded the door, most of them were holding a cup of steaming liquid in their hands: Vino Caliente. Music and loud entertainment filled the whole street.

When entering it became very narrow and even louder. The music group consisted of five musicians in traditional colorful robes, two played the quena, a Peruvian pan flute in different sizes, one had a small flute, one played the ukulele, which they call Charranga here, and finally one sat on a box with a membrane, the cajon, on which the rhythm is beaten. All five took turns singing. The typical music of the Andes is often worn and a bit melancholic, but also has many very rhythmic songs, which were preferred in this environment. The communication was not easy at this noise level, but with the support of Teresa I managed to get a round of Vino caliente. We shared some tapas for this. After 1 hour at the latest in this crowd and the noise level, one is exhausted and simply glad to be back on the street. Teresa and I managed to exchange addresses and phone numbers despite the difficult conditions. Would the promise of Machu Picchu be fulfilled, and this day become the birthday of a lifelong friendship? With this thought in mind we said goodbye for now, not without announcing mutual letters - e-mail and smartphones had not yet been invented. The whole group stood there and had fun with us. I then asked them to line up in a row for a farewell hug. This is how it happened and there was a lot of laughter.

On the way to my simple hotel I walked a little bit through the dark and partly quite lonely alleys, in some of them you can still admire the magnificent walls of the Incas. The big stone blocks of which these walls consist are not uniform and square, but manifold with partly up to seven or eight edges. They were cut so perfectly to fit by the craftsmen of the time with simple tools that they form stable walls without gaps and without mortar, which have even withstood earthquakes over the centuries.

Puerto Maldonado - gateway to the jungle

Cusco is the tourist hotspot of Peru, probably because of this there are a lot of small travel agencies that offer excursions in the surroundings but also flights. It is only a short 45-minute flight from Cusco to Puerto Maldonado, and you are already in the tropical rainforest of the Amazon region. The city lies at the confluence of the Rio Tambopota and the Rio Madre de Dios, one of the main tributaries to the Amazon. On the recently well-constructed road, a section of the new Transoceanica, the journey from Cusco takes at least 6 hours, back then it would have been more like 10 hours or more. The settlement originated in the rubber era, later gold panning and logging were added and currently ecotourism is increasing. Timber processing and especially gold panning using mercury are extremely environmentally harmful activities in the Amazon region, the spread of which is still increasing due to the new Transoceanica from Lima to Rio de Janeiro. On the other hand, in the immediate vicinity of the city are important national parks, which also provide the basis for ecotourism.

So, the 4-day tour into the jungle booked in Cusco led me first by flight to Puerto Maldonado. The old four-engine DC8 came to a sparking halt on the relatively short runway with a perceived emergency stop. From Puerto Maldonado I continued by boat to a lonely lodge in the middle of the rainforest. The lodge was still quite new, the accommodation in small huts with two beds each and a shower amazingly comfortable. Mosquito nets were stretched over the beds, which is indispensable in this area. Electricity was only available for dinner from a generator, otherwise one was dependent on candles and flashlights. Drinking water was available from the barrel, the showers, wash basins and toilets were operated with rarely filtered river water of the Rio Madre de Dios. I had realized the danger that lay in it too late and apparently missed to keep my mouth carefully closed while showering. The result was bacterial dysentery, which I only kept under control with a strong dose of antibiotics on the continuation of my journey - a less good memory of my first jungle experience, but an important lesson for further journeys. Every morning and afternoon there were excursions into the jungle, sometimes on foot in rubber boots, sometimes by boat. The most beautiful was to roam alone through the forest with the local guide, monkeys, snakes, different kinds of parrots and many other birds were our companions. The locals are skilled in observing, they saw animals that I would never have noticed even at a distance. My guide once spotted a scorpion, which was waiting for us on our trail almost 5 m ahead of us. We then avoided him. The most frequent companions on our hikes were rather undesirable, the mosquitoes.

After the overall genuinely nice memories of this trip I planned to visit this lodge again, maybe ten years later, this time together with my wife Cecilia. And there I had to experience how quickly an originally beautiful facility can decay in the tropical humid climate and the rampant jungle if it is not regularly maintained. Obviously, the maintenance had not taken place and so the plant was in a bad condition. The wooden walkways between the huts, the huts themselves and the furnishing of the common rooms, everything made a very rotten impression. The mosquito nets were dirty, and the wooden floors of the showers were covered with a slippery layer of mould on which one did not want to stand with bare feet. We left this place prematurely.

This trip was also not under a good star from the beginning. Cecilia was already affected by altitude sickness in Cusco and during the excursions to the Valle Sagrada and Machu Picchu, she suffered from dizziness and persistent nausea. Apparently not a few tourists do so, especially when they arrive in Lima at sea level after a strenuous flight and then continue their journey to the high-altitude Cusco. We could observe this in the evening in a restaurant very drastically at a Japanese travel group. It was obviously their first evening, immediately after the long flight from Japan and the connecting flight to Cusco. Half of the groups fell asleep before dinner was served, the others looked miserable, one of them had to throw up. I would have liked to have given Cecilia more beautiful impressions on her first trip to Peru. Because of her altitude sickness I changed the itinerary at short notice. A planned side trip to the highlands of Bolivia was cancelled, instead we went directly to Arequipa and later to Lima a few days earlier than planned. Then we have also broken off this journey, in the end, prematurely.

Luckily, there were two more trips to Peru with Cecilia in later years, which were pleasant and more in keeping with the beauty of the country. Also, to Puerto Maldonado I should go again, together with my friend and photographer Peter, but more about that later. First, we go back to the beginning of my travels.

Arequipa - the beautiful white city

Already on my first trip to Peru I did not want to miss Arequipa, according to many travel-guides the most beautiful city of Peru. This refers in particular to the beautiful big Plaza de Armas in the middle of the old town, which can surely be called the most beautiful place in Peru. It is also noticeable that most of the houses in the city center are built of the volcanic white sillar stone, which is why Arequipa is also called Ciudad blanca, the white city. Arequipa is the capital of the province of the same name and is considered the economic and cultural center of southern Peru. The city with about 55,000 inhabitants is in a moderate climate zone at an altitude of about 2,300 m. The weather is mostly spring-like. The inhabitants, the Arequipenas, are immensely proud of their city and are considered a bit stuck-up and arrogant in the rest of Peru. They are especially proud of the active volcano El Misti, which is located northeast of the city and has an altitude of 5,822 m. The much sung about and revered volcano with its classic cone shape and snow-covered top had its last eruption in 1985.

Every day there are numerous buses of different companies that connect Lima and Arequipa. The journey from Lima to the south on the Panamericana Sur takes about 17 hours for the 1,000 km. It passes the Pacific coastal towns of Pisco and Ica, as well as the small town of Nazca, known for its long straight stripes on the rocky bottom, whose origin is still unclear. There are wild speculations about this, which suspect landing strips of aliens there. Of course, it is faster to Arequipa by plane in about one and a half hours.

Arriving in Arequipa for the first time I found the inexpensive Hostal Jerusalen on the same named street, six blocks away from the Plaza de Armas, on the recommendation of the South America Handbook, my constant travel companion. My first way then led to the Plaza. The interior of the plaza is planted with a fountain in the middle; with a little luck, one can even find a shady place on the numerous benches and watch the life around one. One sees young and old couples, parents and children, businessmen, seniors, some traders for drinks, chewing gum and lots, as also shoe shiners. Some writers have also set up their typewriters on small tables and offer to help with writing or filling out forms. The whole northern side of the plaza is taken by the front of the huge cathedral of the 17th century. If you look to the right, you can see the snow-covered crater of the volcano El Misti, a unique panorama that contributes greatly to the charm of this square. This panorama is especially beautiful in the dusk, when the plaza and the cathedral are already illuminated, but the white peak of the mountain is still in the evening sun. The view is ideal from the balconies on the sides of the square, where there are some cafés and restaurants. The cathedral was severely damaged by fire and earthquake in the 19th century and had to be partially rebuilt. On a later trip I could experience the Easter procession in and in front of this cathedral, an important and very impressive event in the predominantly catholic city of Arequipa.

On my walk through the surroundings of the Plaza I came across an old flat but beautifully designed and ornamentally decorated building with a majestic entrance that suggested an important function of the building. While I was still trying to figure out this function, I noticed that I was being watched. From the large window next to the entrance, two young women looked out and were obviously amused by my efforts. I addressed them in English and asked them for information about the building. One of them answered me and explained that it was the law department of the Universidad Nacional de San Augustin de Arequipa. She, Grace, and her friend Maria were law students at that university. I invited them both for a coffee and a portion of ice cream, and so we went to a café on the balcony of the plaza. Grace was lively, eloquent, and obviously enjoyed questioning the foreign tourist thoroughly. She came from Arequipa and spoke English quite well. Maria, on the other hand, was rather reserved, the conversation with her was also difficult for me, as she only spoke Spanish. And my Spanish was limited to ordering a meal in the restaurant and asking for a room in the hotel. But I liked her, the slim young woman with brown skin and long black hair.

Grace helped with translations, and so I found out that Maria came from Tacna, the southernmost city of Peru right on the border with Chile, 370 km or 5 hours by bus from Arequipa. I liked both, and so we exchanged addresses, which resulted in many years of correspondence with them. And I should see both again - on later visits in Arequipa.

However, I have not only good memories to report about Arequipa. During one of my later visits here, what probably many tourists in South America experience, I was robbed. And that in a bank while changing money. Of course, there was also carelessness involved, I carried my essential valuables in one of the then modern wrist bags. This should not happen to an experienced traveler; one always carries one's valuables close to the body and concealed. So now there was a quick grip from behind and the bag was gone. And with it my return flight ticket (at that time there were only paper tickets), the driver's license, the credit card and my money, except the amount the bank clerk was about to hand over to me together with my passport. A small nimble man was invisible in a flash, and the two policemen positioned at the entrance of the bank and armed with machine guns watched the events idly and with absolute disinterest. My request to do something about it only caused a slight shrug of their shoulders. After all, they gave me the address of the nearest police station with the recommendation to file a report there. This process, which started in the early morning, took the rest of the day. The result was a form which was extremely important for the recovery of the lost documents and which finally even served as a document for my return flight. The stolen credit card was blocked at the American Express office and a replacement card was issued immediately. Fortunately, I had kept my passport, as it was needed for the exchange of money, otherwise there would have been problems when leaving the country. I had learned the lesson of more caution with it, and the fashion for wrist bags was finally dead for me.

Lima - lively capital with tradition

I have always made sure to spend at least one or two full days in Lima before the flight back home from Peru, so that I do not miss the return flight. The transport connections in Peru were not always exceptionally reliable. Flights were cancelled more often, because of the weather, because of defective machines or because of too little utilization. The buses were generally reliable, but even then, road closures, military and police checks or accidents could cause considerable delays or cancellations. Furthermore, Lima is a remarkably interesting city in many respects and the visit is very worthwhile. The old center of Lima is located at the Rio Rimac, which has different amounts of water depending on the season. In general, Lima has an increasing lack of water and the supply from the mountains can hardly meet the growing demand. The central places of the old city, the Plaza de Armas and the Plaza San Martin are connected by the narrow street Jiron de la Union, the main shopping street in this district. Here, in the 80s and 90s, one could buy gold relatively cheaply, and there was a rich supply of gold jewelry and handicrafts. Some beautiful pieces can still be found today in Cecilia's jewelry box. A lot of little boys earn their money by selling chewing gum or as shoeshine boys. In the same street is the oldest Catholic church in town, La Merced, built in 1546 as a monastery church. Not far from the Plaza de Armas is the old baroque monastery church San Francisco, built in 1674, with its famous old choir stalls and numerous paintings by the Spanish artist Francisco de Zubaran. Very impressive is the crypt with the finely sorted bones of about 25,000 citizens of the city, who were buried here before the main cemetery was opened in 1808. At the Plaza de Armas there is the cathedral, today a museum, in which the bones of the conqueror Francisco Pizarro are laid out in a glass coffin. Also, at the Plaza de Armas there is the palace of the president of Peru. At the Plaza San Martin is the traditional Gran Hotel Bolivar, once the best hotel in the city.

Since the beginning of this century, the business and tourist center of the city has moved to the coastal areas of the city, especially to Miraflores. There you can now find the modern high-rise buildings of the big hotel chains, impressive office towers and numerous luxurious shops. While the markets of the city offer simple blankets, ponchos and sweaters made of alpaca wool, the shops of Miraflores offer finer clothes made of the noble material, specially of baby alpaca wool, and this at quite reasonable prices.
A steep rock face leads from the city down to the Pacific Ocean, where sports fields and beaches alternate. On the upper promenade there are nice little parks and

shopping malls, especially the nicely located Larcomar with many shops and restaurants overlooking the Pacific Ocean. Surfers ride the waves and motorized kites glide along the coast and use the upwind for their maneuvers, so the view never gets boring.

Christmas in Chiclayo

After a regular exchange of letters with Teresa following our meeting in Cusco, she invited me to visit her family - even over Christmas. I was overly excited to see what Christmas would be like there and I was happy to have the opportunity to experience this in a family. My tight budget allowed only the cheapest flight - and that was Avianca from Düsseldorf via Paris, Madrid, Caracas, Bogota to Lima, and then the Peruvian airline Faucett to Chiclayo in northern Peru, where Teresa lives. All in all, I travelled almost 40 hours with this adventurous connection. Arriving at Chiclayo airport I was welcomed by the whole family. We did not know each other yet, except Teresa, but they had looked at photos of me. Teresa has two younger siblings, a sister, and an even younger brother. The first one who recognized me was Teresa's little brother. He stormed towards me, grabbed my travel-bag, and ran off with it. And of course, I thought he had just stolen my bag! As I was about to run after him to get my bag back, I saw him running towards Teresa, who I recognized immediately. After this first fright there was a warm welcome from the whole family and a happy reunion with Teresa. We drove with the family car to her house, a terraced house in a quiet street near the city center, where the closer family lived on the two upper floors. The lower floors were inhabited by relatives.

Teresa was extremely excited, talked like a waterfall and asked me about everything and anything. It was nice to be welcomed so warmly, but I was much too tired after the long journey to really enjoy it and to tell a lot. Teresa's mother noticed this and after a small meal she admonished her daughter to let me sleep and showed me my room. I spent the next 12 hours in a deep sleep in bed.

Christmas on December 24th was indeed quite different from what I was used to at home. That already started with the climate. Peru is in the southern hemisphere of the earth and it is summer there in December. The temperatures in Chiclayo can be 30° or more during the day in this season. So, we went to the beach in the morning. This beach is located near the small village of Pimentel, just 12 km away from Chiclayo. The afternoon, back at the house, was terribly busy and a bit chaotic. The reason was an enormous evening buffet, which was prepared in the kitchen in community work. I had not expected such a rich meal on Christmas Eve here, I am also rather used to a modest meal on Christmas Eve and the feast is then on Christmas Day. The evening came and the whole family sat together while the last preparations were still going on. As you know it from America there was a rather small artificial Christmas tree, which was richly decorated and with many colorful lamps. I had brought a few modest Christmas presents with me, which I then put on the table. Teresa's father thanked me on behalf of the family and made a toast to the German guest. With the good food, the mood rose, it was loud, people talked in disarray and there was a lot of laughter. Music was added, the Christmas carols are less melancholic than the German ones, and in between there were also lively South American rhythms, such as salsa. There was dancing. Now I am rather a bad dancer, and probably most South Americans, including Teresa, are enthusiastic and good dancers. So, I embarrassed myself heartily in this company. Nevertheless, I was able to enjoy the dancing skills of my young friend. The doors to the street were open and occasionally neighbors came by to wish a Merry Christmas. It was getting late.

In Teresa's family I was able to experience great hospitality. I was shown the city of Chiclayo, a famous historical museum in the neighboring town of Lambayeque and the large dam project Tinajones, which was supported by Germany. The Royal Tombs of Sipan Museum in Lambayeque, 15 km north of Chiclayo, shows - directly next to the sites - artistic grave goods of the royal tombs of Sipan from the pre-Inca time. Further finds are shown in the neighboring Museo Arqueologico Nacional Brüning. The reservoir of Tinajones was almost empty at this time and the ground was dried out. At the edge of the reservoir we found some mango trees. We climbed up, sat down on the branches and Teresa showed me how to eat mangos out of the hand without getting terrible stains. Then in a restaurant it came to a situation that seriously touched me. The family ordered a plate of rice with a sauce for everyone, only on my plate there was a chicken leg. My protest was not accepted, also Teresa refused a division. I had to accept this act of hospitality, although it embarrassed me. Probably the household cash box was simply empty after the sumptuous Christmas dinner.

After the beautiful Christmas days in Chiclayo my plan for the next stage was to continue by bus to Huaraz. I offered Teresa to come along with me, which her parents of course would not allow. So, after a few nice days I had a warm farewell at the bus station and for me alone the start of my new stage.

The white peaks of the Andes

With the trip to Huaraz I came for the first time to the mountainous region of the province Ancash. It is a large province in the northern half of Peru, which is home to some of the highest mountains in the Andes as well as 220 kilometers of Peru's Pacific coast. About 1 million people live in Ancash. The capital of the province, with a modest 55,000 inhabitants, is Huaraz, located about 350 kilometers north of Lima on the edge of the Cordillera Blanca, the high mountain region of the Andes with mountains up to 6,700 meters high. Chimbote, the largest city in the province with 180,000 inhabitants, is located on the Pacific coast and is known for its fish processing industry, which is immediately noticeable by its intense aroma when passing through.

The bus drove south on the Panamericana to Casma. There I had to change to another bus after a waiting period, which left the Panamericana on smaller roads to the east towards Cordillera Blanca. At the station I ordered a beer and got a 1-liter bottle, good for the fluid balance in the heat and for the rest during the following night drive to Huaraz. In the early morning, the bus reached the bus station there. It was bitterly cold, Huaraz is at an altitude of 3,000 m and there is often night frost. The town is small, pretty, and relatively quiet, from higher situated districts you have a wonderful view to the snow-covered peaks of the Cordillera Blanca. After a really cold night in the un-heated room of my small hostel, only equipped with a thin blanket, I bought a nice alpaca blanket the next morning at the market, which I carried with me from then on during my further journey. But it kept me wonderfully warm in the cold of the mountain land-scape, and I was still sometimes glad that I had it with me. From Huaraz you can make wonderful tours into the high mountains, but that needs time for planning and preparation and the appropriate equipment too. On the other hand, I wanted to go to the south of the country and so I looked for a cheap bus connection for the 8-hour trip to Lima. However, I should return to the exciting landscapes of the province of Ancash several times during later trips.

New Year's Eve in Lima

The year was coming to an end, I had arrived well in Lima and had found a cheap accommodation in the old city center. And so, I stood on the central Plaza San Martin in the early New Year's Eve and wondered if there might be some midnight fireworks. It did not make me suspicious when two young women approached and addressed me. It happened more often for me as a single traveler, especially in restaurants, that I was curiously addressed where I came from. Such a question was not considered "racist" at that time, and I always found it simply curious interest, never disturbing. That is how it was here, a conversation developed, and I was quite happy not to be standing there alone. Finally, the two asked me if I would like to go to a nearby disco with them to celebrate New Year's Eve. Well, I had nothing else planned. So, we left, and on the way two friends joined us. It got me thinking. Then we reached the queue in front of the entrance of the discotheque, more people joined us, who obviously knew my companions as well. They talked and although I did not understand much, I soon realized that I was supposed to play the role of the golden donkey for a larger group. So, I made myself heard, said goodbye with a few friendly words and my thanks for the companionship so far and wished everyone a happy New Year's Eve. Then I quickly left the field, the golden donkey became a greyhound. Many disappointed faces showed me that I was not completely wrong with my assumption. I spent the rest of the New Year's Eve in my hotel room, and there were no fireworks on the Plaza San Martin either.

Trip from Chiclayo to Ecuador

In the following years I got the chance to visit Teresa several times in her house with her family. The next visit took place a little later. I arrived in Chiclayo by bus at noon, and since I already knew the address and the house I went there directly. However, nobody was at home, and because I did not feel like walking through the city with my travel bag, I decided without further ado to throw it over the railing onto the small balcony on the first floor. The second throw succeeded. Then I went to the Plaza de Armas, sat down on a bench in the shade and watched the place and the hustle and bustle of the people. In the late afternoon I went back to the house and found the family present and rather surprised about my missing luggage. I explained everything and Teresa's little brother came triumphantly from the balcony with my travel bag. Afterwards I had to listen to a sermon, however, that something like that does not work at all in Peru and I should be glad that the bag was still there. I was not aware of any guilt, but one was right - another lesson learned! Unfortunately Teresa's father had left the family in the meantime because of another relationship, and so on this second visit I experienced a meanwhile very grown up and independent Teresa who drove through the city in the family car and very confidently continued her father's business, a car accessory shop. Her godfather partially replaced her father as padrino. However, the young woman's independence ended due to the partly rigid Peruvian customs and traditions. When I wanted to go to a disco with Teresa one evening, her mother and the padrino came along as a matter of course and watched us. Under this strict supervision, the first kiss, which was due and expected by both sides, unfortunately had to miss. It had to wait a little longer.

During this second visit to Chiclayo I extended an invitation to Teresa to come and visit me for a longer period in front of the family, which did not arouse spontaneous enthusiasm in her mother. But in fact, Teresa came to Düsseldorf after some time for a 3-week visit - her first trip abroad. A little later she married and had two children. I visited her and her family twice later in Chiclayo, once with Cecilia and once with our son Abdon.

From Chiclayo my journey continued by bus over the Panamericana to the north. Shortly after the next town, Lambayeque, the Panamericana forks into an eastern branch along the Andes and a western branch along the coast. On the western branch, which the long-distance buses take because the route is much faster, the journey begins shortly after the fork on a straight stretch through the desert, right and left of the road only sand as far as you can see. After 215km and 3 hours driving the bus reaches the next bigger city, Piura. The city, located at the small Rio Piura, was founded in 1532 by Francisco Pizarro as the first Spanish city in Peru with the name San Miguel de Piura, a little bit away from the present city. The Rio Piura, which is a fertile ribbon in the desert, flows into the Pacific Ocean about 60km west. Today Piura has more than 150.000 inhabitants and is the sixth largest city in Peru. The Plaza de Armas is a nice place because you can find shady seats under the many old trees. At the head of the square is the baroque cathedral from 1588. In the evening, according to my impression, the square becomes a meeting place for the whole youth of the city, carefully styled, loud and with lots of music, preferably from the loudspeakers of pimped up cars.

Further north on the Panamericana, the dry desert heat soon gives way to a humid tropical climate with increasing vegetation. In the Reserva Nacional de Tumbes there is already dense forest and a ramified network of small rivers. Tumbes is the last major city before the Ecuadorian border, and - together with Iquitos on the Amazon - one of the two northernmost cities in Peru, and therefore closest to the equator. The direct crossing of the border by long-distance bus on the Panamericana was temporarily not possible at that time because Peru and Ecuador were in a political conflict due to some oil fields in the Amazon region. So, the bus ended in Tumbes, then we continued with regional buses to the small border town of Aguas Verdes. Over the border river Rio Zanumilla goes the Puente Internacional Peru-Ecuador, which we had to cross on foot to complete the border formalities. On the other side, in Ecuador, there were again regional buses to the next bigger city, Machala, ready. From there we continued with the big long-distance buses to Guayaquil, the second largest city and most important port of Ecuador. Probably I do the today's city Guayaquil very wrong, and probably I have also at that time spent the night in the wrong quarter, because I have experienced this city as not very beautiful, not very clean and rather dangerous. Anyway, I took - in the truest sense of the word - "the next train" to get out of this city again. Yes, there is indeed a railway line in Ecuador, and it goes from Duran to the capital Quito in the middle of the Andes. Duran is located from Guayaquil on the other side of the Rio Guayas, exactly at the point where the two rivers Rio Daule and Rio Babahayo join to form this river. Thus, one only must cross two bridges to arrive in Duran directly at the train station.

The railway line between Guayaquil and Quito was built at the end of the 19th century. The line is very demanding for a railway construction, between the two cities there are about 3.000 altitude meters to overcome. Especially for an ascent on a rock face, the so-called Nariz del Diabolo (Devil's Nose), the 500 m difference in altitude there could only be overcome with a zigzag course over several turns. The first train reached the capital Quito on 25 June 1908. The railway line has a very changeable and eventful history. Especially due to heavy rainfalls in the Andes the tracks were often damaged and were temporarily impassable on some parts of the line.

At the time I was there, the train could only drive on the line from Guayaquil to Riobamba. The remaining 200 km to Quito needed a change to a bus. But at least the most interesting passage, the Devil's Nose, was within the passable distance. So, I took the train to Riobamba. The first part of the journey goes through dense tropical vegetation, pineapple and banana plantations caught my eye. With increasing altitude, the vegetation becomes sparser and sparser and the impressive rocky landscape prevails. The hunger came up and I bought a bundle of bananas from a boy at a station. I opened a banana, wanted to bite into it and noticed that it was rock hard. That way I learned that there are also plantains - another lesson. The grin and laughter of the Ecuadorians around me could not get out of my head for a long time.

Since the time of the flight home was getting closer, I decided to do without the further bus trip to Quito and took a bus in the other direction to Cuenca instead. I should see Quito several times on later occasions. The provincial capital Cuenca, originally called Santa Ana de los Cuatro Rios de Cuenca, was a nice, rather quiet little university town at that time. Today it is the third largest city of Ecuador with about 350,000 inhabitants. Situated in the middle of the southern Andes of Ecuador, it offers a pleasant climate at an altitude of about 2,500 m, which is pleasantly different from the sultry heat in Guayaquil. Landmark of the city is the huge cathedral, which is said to hold 10,000 believers. Due to the frequent earthquakes in this area, the completion of a church tower was renounced as a precaution. From Cuenca it is only a good 100 km further to Machala and from there in the already known procedure back to Peru and to Tumbes. There I took a long-distance bus and reached Lima on time after about 18 hours. The flight home was secured.

Trujillo - the dusty cultural capital

If one drives from Lima by bus along the Panamericana to the north in direction to Chiclayo, then the next bigger city Chimbote, the biggest city of the district Ancash, is recognizable by the penetrating smell of the fish factories. Further north is Trujillo, the capital of the La Libertad district. Trujillo is located on the Pacific coast and has about 350,000 inhabitants. It is named after the Spanish city Trujillo, the birthplace of Francisco Pizarro. The city is considered the cultural capital of Peru and suffers from high crime rates. Adjacent to the city to the west, between the city and the airport, lies the historic city of Chan Chan, the capital of the pre-Columbian Chimu Empire.

The bus stopped not far from the Plaza de Armas, and as always on my first visit to a Peruvian city, I asked for the Plaza, which is usually also the center of the city. In the center of the Plaza de Armas there is a monumental statue of liberty that reminds on the declaration of independence of Peru in the year 1820 that was proclaimed here. At the head of the plaza is the Basilica of St. Mary, which was built around 1650 as the mother church of the local archbishopric, after earlier churches on this site were destroyed by earthquakes. In the immediate proximity of the plaza I found a small but quite comfortable hotel, where I deposited my luggage and returned to the plaza after a first impression of the city. I sat down on a shady place and let the colorful hustle and bustle around me take effect on me. It was the typical mixture of strollers, couples, salesmen, shoeshine boys and such businessmen who were always correctly dressed in a dark suit even in the afternoon heat. And as so often on such occasions, I was curiously glanced at by three young women who obviously enjoyed my very casual travel outfit. Finally, one of them dared to speak to me and introduced herself as Consuelo. A little hesitant the other two then joined us. After the usual first few minutes of interviewing, I bought a round of ice cream and lemonade or coffee at the next café to relax. Afterwards they wanted to show me the city. And indeed, it was very worthwhile. Trujillo is not only a popular tourist destination because of its historical sites, but also because of its colonial town villas with beautiful courtyards, wooden balconies, and wrought-iron window grills.

Consuelo had a remarkably interesting privilege for me, she was allowed to drive her father's old VW Beetle. And so, we arranged for the next morning to go on a city tour and a joint trip for four with her Beetle to the ruins of Chan Chan. And indeed, they stood punctually (!) in front of my hotel, all three of them, and Consuelo proudly presented me her VW Beetle. Then we drove off. Even in the outskirts Trujillo is a very dusty city, after all it is literally in a desert and often there is a fresh breeze from the nearby coast. It is not far to drive to Chan Chan, the historical site is located directly on the outskirts of the city on the way to the airport.

Chan Chan, built around 850 as the capital of the Chimu culture, was probably the largest city in America at that time. It was built entirely of mud bricks, which were well preserved in the dryness of the region. Chan Chan was conquered by the Incas in 1470 and finally destroyed by the Spaniards in the 16th century with the simultaneous founding of the city of Trujillo. Apart from the complex uncovered by excavations, the temple Huaca El Dragon, which probably belongs to Chan Chan, is located a little aside and in the middle of the city area of Trujillo. Even bigger and even older are two buildings on the east side of the city that we visited afterwards. They are the temples Huaca del Sol (sun temple) and Huaca de la Luna (moon temple), enormously large buildings also made of mud bricks from the Moche culture, which settled this area from the 1st to the 8th century and is considered as predecessor of the Chimu culture.

After this impressive sightseeing we drove to Consuelo's home, where I also got to know her parents. There was again alternatively coffee or lemonade and many curious questions, until I said goodbye with many thanks for the guided tours and for the hospitality. Later, I still had letter contact with Consuelo for a while.

Iquitos - and a military reception

Iquitos, the mysterious city on the Amazon River, to which no continuous road leads, has long been one of my desired destinations in Peru. The capital of the province of Maynas with a population of 150,000 inhabitants can only be reached by river or by plane, there is no overland route through the jungle. Iquitos is located in the north-eastern tip of Peru near the borders to Colombia and Brazil. About 50 km north and downstream the Rio Napo, which comes from Ecuador, flows into the Amazon. Two other small rivers flow into the Amazon near Iquitos, the Rio Nanay in the north of the city and the Rio Maranon in the south. The city was founded around 1750 as a mission of the Jesuit, which was elevated to the status of Apostolic Prefecture in 1900 and Apostolic Vicariate in 1921. Between 1870 and 1900 the rubber trade boomed and let arise numerous splendid, partly colorfully painted mansions in the city center. Around 1960 Iquitos began to develop into a rich and modern city through the extraction of oil, the timber industry and later through tourism.

I took the plane from the capital Lima, 1.100 km away. On the approach to the small international airport, all you can see is dense forest and the meandering course of the rivers. As in every bigger Peruvian city, the Plaza de Armas is in the center of the city, the biggest square with the cathedral, which is also the highest building of the city here. And right by the square is the city's most famous mansion, the so-called Iron House, Casa de Fierro, designed by Gustave Eiffel in his own style. More critical was the visit to the Belen district on the Rio Maranon. Houses and footbridges stand on high stilts because the water of the river can rise up to 10 m in a rainy period. Here live the mostly impoverished Indians and in addition on this muddy ground is a big market for food, exotic animals and all kinds of jungle medicine and voodoo articles. A colorful mixture of various and mostly unpleasant smells as well as all sorts of running, crawling and flying creatures and a suspected armada of pickpockets, however, make little desire to buy food and also let the stay on this market not become unnecessarily long.

I found a cheap room in the Holiday Inn Hotel and, as it was strongly advised against nightly walks in the city, I decided to spend the evening with my South American Handbook and a glass of wine at the hotel bar. There was decent music and some couples danced, and as a few stools further on a young woman was also sitting alone at the bar, I asked her if she wanted to dance. Now, I am not a very gifted dancer, but it was enough to get into conversation, she even spoke good English. I found out that her name is Diana and that she is a friend of a higher officer of the Peruvian Navy who was doing an exercise with his unit in the Amazon. After we got to know each other a bit better, she offered me to come with her the next morning to the Naval Camp and meet her friend. Sure he would be happy, she said.

Her insurance still a little bit incredulous in my ear I expected her after breakfast in the hotel lobby. We left and reached the camp at the river, where a bigger transport ship and several small speedboats had moored and about 30 soldiers were present. To my surprise the officer was really happy and gave me a warm welcome. He had his men lined up and welcomed me as a German guest in his camp. Now, military rituals are quite foreign to me, but I was good enough for a strapping posture and a few friendly words in Spanish, and these were complaisantly received. Diana stood on the edge and added a sphinx-like smile. The officer then took Diana and me and a soldier to his speedboat and we set off, down the Amazon. The soldier steered the boat and the officer gave me some explanations about the border protection in the region and the special strategic location of Iquitos. He spoke clearly and not too fast, so I could understand him quite well. Diana and I enjoyed the beautiful tour on the Amazon.

After about an hour we reached the camp again. I thanked the officer for his warm hospitality and said goodbye to him and Diana. The Sphinx smiled and kept silent. Back to the city I had to walk a long way, a taxi was not to be seen far and wide. The rest of the day I continued to look around in tropical Iquitos. One of the short but very heavy downpours typical for the afternoon drove me on the shortest way to the next café and soon out into the beautiful fresh tropical air after the rain. I spent the evening again with my South American Handbook and a glass of wine, Diana was not to be seen anymore. The next morning, I went to the airport and back to Lima.

By train through Peru

There are two railway lines in Peru, one of them is the Ferrocaril Central Andino, which runs from Lima across the heights of the Central Andes to the city of Huancayo. For the distance of 332 km the train needs 10-14 hours. Huancayo is located at an altitude of 3,260 m, on the way there the train must cross a mountain pass with more than 4,800 m altitude. There is also the highest station, Galera with 4.781 m. The impressive mountain route goes over seven hairpin bends, 60 bridges and 66 tunnels and leads over the whole length through an impressive mountain land-scape. Since not all passengers can stand this altitude well and then suffer from altitude sickness (soroche), the train is always accompanied by a nurse and oxy-gen bottles are also available.

Currently the train only runs twice a month. The jour-ney is also much more expensive than with the com-fortable long-distance buses, which cover the distance much faster in about 8 hours.

I had decided to take the train only as far as La Oroya, which is almost two thirds of the distance to Huancayo. In La Oroya at an altitude of 3.750 m the train meets another train in the opposite direction, so I could do the return trip in one day. This certainly worked, as the two trains had to wait for each other on the largely single-track line in La Oroya. The train ride started in Lima at around 7:00 a.m. at the historic Desamperados station, which is in the immediate vi-cinity of the Plaza de Armas, i.e. in the old city center. A brass band bid farewell to the train shortly before departure. I had already bought the tickets a few days before in a travel agency; today, this is also possible via internet, and because of the now rarely running trains, a very early booking is recommended. The average speed of the train is about 40km/h, so it goes very slowly. In addition, there are many stops, where sometimes the locomotive is changed. Food and drinks are served in the train, but the most beautiful thing is of course the view. On the adventurous single-track railway, we first follow the Rio Rimac along a canyon and parallel to the road Ruta 22 steadily up-hill. Rugged cliffs frame the gorge, only down by the river there is vegetation. Tunnels and bridges alternate, and some ascents can only be managed in zig-zag.

In La Oroya I changed to the other train back towards Lima, which was already waiting on another track. While the train was rolling downhill through the valley, I enjoyed the magnificent mountain scenery again on the way back. A few rows of seats in front of me in the carriage I noticed a pretty younger couple who looked more European than the other passengers. They were talking in a language I could not identify, but still understood a few words of it. Curious, I approached them and got to know Randi and Jostein from Norway. We got into conversation and exchanged our travel plans and experiences. Randi and Jostein were on their way by train from Huancayo to Lima. They were in Peru for the first time and still had some destinations for their onward journey. Among others they wanted to go to Cusco and Arequipa. Arequipa was still on my travel plan too because I had an appointment with Grace and Maria there. We compared our routes and found out that Randi and Jostein had booked a flight to Cusco for the next morning just like me. After arriving in Lima, a dinner together rounded off the nice getting to know each other. In Cusco we met again the next day and arranged to have dinner again. Then our ways separated at first. Randi and Jostein had Machu Picchu and the Valle Sagrado in their sights and I wanted to take another train connection from Cusco to Lake Titicaca and then to Arequipa. But we decided to meet there as well and arranged a meeting for a certain day at 12:00 noon at the Plaza de Armas.

The second Peruvian railway line, Ferrocaril del Sur, leads from Cusco to Lago Titicaca up to Juliaca, the neighboring city of Puno, which is located directly at the lake. The line then continues via Arequipa to the Pacific coast to the port of Malarani. This oldest part of the line, built by the German engineer Friedrich Blume, was put into operation as early as 1870, the connection to Cusco followed in 1908. The original purpose of the railway was to transport agricultural products and rocks containing copper or silver from the highlands for shipment across the Pacific. Today the railway is mainly used for tourism. This also attracts all sorts of professionals from the theft trade as fellow travelers, so that this railway has a reputation for stealing from most travelers during their journey. For example, the cutting of luggage with razors is supposedly exceedingly popular. Beside this old PeruRail train there is also a super luxury train, the Belmond Andean Explorer, which leaves nothing to be desired, with a panorama terrace, star cook and champagne bar and a lot of service, medical and security personnel.

This luxury train did not exist yet, when I boarded the simple train in Cusco, at the station Estacion del Sur Wanchaq, which should bring me in (officially) about

10 hours over the 380 km to Juliaca. This train was much less comfortable than the train from Lima to Huancayo. And it started late and collected another two hours delay on the way, so that it reached Juliaca only in the evening. I took good care of my luggage and luckily had no problem with the gangs of thieves. The bigger problem was the condition of the toilets, so filthy that you really could not enter the rooms. Somehow, I managed to get through the 12 hours without using them. The route is as adventurous and scenic as the one from Lima to La Oroya. The highest point is at the pass La Raya with 4.314 m, where the train stops at a small station. Around 20:30 o'clock it finally reached Juliaca. There is also a branch line to Puno from there, but at this time of day there was no train scheduled, so I had to look for a bus to reach my destination Puno at Lago Titicaca.

The Titicaca Lake

The bus station near the train station was dark, crowded, and noisy, and certainly a place where you should keep an eye on your luggage with special care. I noticed a younger couple who had got off the train with me; the woman was probably Peruana and was already negotiating with police and bus drivers, apparently, they did not want to stay in Juliaca either. The man looked European with his blond hair and so I asked him where to continue his journey. It turned out that both wanted to go on to Puno and the woman was just looking for the right bus. So, I got to know Martha and Winfried, she Peruana from Chiclayo and he German, they lived together in Konstanz and for him it was also the first trip to her home country Peru. It was a stroke of luck for me to continue the journey with Martha and Winfried because the difficulties were just beginning in Puno. When the bus had finally made the 40 km to Puno, we heard from a taxi driver that the quarters in the city were practically booked out. Nevertheless, we entered the taxi and asked the driver to take us to some quarters to at least try to find a place to stay for the night. It seemed almost hopeless, at least ten requests were without result and we had already left the city. Finally, we found a hostel, in which we were offered the last two small rooms. It was done, not least because of Martha's negotiating skills. With all the luck to finally find a room with a bed and washing facilities, I found out that the bed inside was anything but clean. I quickly covered it up again and preferred to sleep fully clothed on the blanket. Despite of the cold I had put my jacket over the pillow as a precaution. It became an uncomfortable night, but still better than somewhere outside. Martha and Winfried had been a little better off but were not exactly happy with our accommodation either. The next morning, we searched and found a better hostel for the next night.

Puno is with about 125,000 inhabitants the capital of the province with the same name, beautifully situated directly at the Lago Titicaca at 3,800 m altitude. To the city also belongs a port for the traffic to the islands and to the neighboring Bolivia on the other side of the lake. A mighty cathedral from the 17th century is located on one side of the largest square, the Plaza de Armas, as in many places in Peru. At the harbor and in the city center there are some nice daily markets. Some small islands with very few inhabitants belong to the city. Other islands, built only of reed, belong to the Indian tribe of the Uros, who live only on Lake Titicaca and live from the lake and the reed that serves them as food and from which their boats are also made. The islands need constant renewal so that they do not become saturated with water and sink after some time. They can also be visited by tourists, so I booked a boat trip to the Uros. Indian handicrafts are offered on the islands, the income from the tourists is the only source of money for the Indians besides possible governmental support.

Once at Lago Titicaca, I decided to take the opportunity to cross the lake to the Bolivian side and then continue to La Paz. The crossing was quite uncomfortable and bumpy with an old Russian hydrofoil boat, but in breathtaking speed. On the other side, after the appropriate entry controls, we continued by bus to La Paz. The city lies at a base altitude of almost 3,800 m picturesquely between mountain peaks that rise far above it. Some districts are located on the slopes or on higher plateaus. To walk the city on foot is very exhausting at this altitude, as it is continuously going up and down. I stayed there only one day and took the speedboat back across the lake to Peru.

Appointments in Arequipa

But now I had to make sure to get to Arequipa quickly, because there I had an appointment with Randi and
Jostein and with Maria and Grace. I chose the fastest
and most comfortable way to get there and took the
bus. The bus took about 6 hours for the 300 km on the
then still partly unpaved road including a pass crossing. The next day, the day of my appointments, I saw
Randi and Jostein standing on the Plaza de Armas at
noon, and we could celebrate our reunion together in
one of the cafés on the balconies. I was able to treat
some slight health problems of the two of them with
appropriate medicine from my extensive travel phar-
macy. On this occasion they also got to know Grace
and Maria, and it did not escape them that I was interested in Maria, although the communication with my
meanwhile better but still quite marginal Spanish
knowledge was difficult. Together we visited some
sightseeing of the beautiful city, specially the Monas-
terio de Santa Catalina, not far from the Plaza de Armas. In the convent that was founded in 1579, up to
150 nuns of the order of Saint Catherine of Siena lived
there. In the year 1970, the recently renovated convent
was opened to the public in a big part; a few nuns still
live in a separated wing of the complex. The convent
looks like a Spanish miniature city, with furnished
rooms, paintings and equipped kitchens. The streets
are named after Spanish cities and the houses are
painted in orange, dark red or blue, some of them also

white. Several small places loosen up the picture of the big settlement.

Randi and Jostein wanted to travel on, and I stayed two days longer. Maria suggested to take a tour together to the Valle de Colca, a deep gorge where the condor of the Andes can often be seen. So, I booked a day tour for us in a travel agency, and early in the morning we set off on the rather bumpy 6-hour drive with a minibus to the Cruz del Condor viewpoint on a hill of the canyon. The Valle de Colca is supposedly the deepest canyon in the world - as well as some others, for example in the USA, Mexico and Greece. The view into the canyon is really spectacular and remarkable; and in the very distance we could also make out two big birds, maybe they were Andean condors. Unfortunately, they did not come closer to us. After a two-hour stop the bus driver urged us to return, and in the late evening we reached Arequipa again.

After our encounters in Peru, I continued to correspond with Randi and Jostein in casual correspondence until a few years later I decided to visit them in Norway with Cecilia. The visit began with a big surprise, since Randi and Jostein had firmly assumed that I was married to Maria and were therefore quite surprised to meet Cecilia, an Asian, when they welcomed me. But this was quickly cleared up and it was a genuinely nice get-together in the Norwegian town of Forde - and the beginning of a wonderful and warm friendship. Since then we have been visiting each other every year, alternately in Norway and in Germany, and sometimes together completely elsewhere, e.g. in the Philippines.

A lecture tour with adventure

I do not remember exactly how it happened, but in a fit of high spirits I had promised Maria to give a lecture at her university. She was proud to have me as a foreign lecturer at her university. But she was studying law, so of course it had to be a legal subject. I had been involved in environmental protection for many years, and by working as the managing director of the German Society for Noise Abatement (DAL) I had finally financed my medical studies. Legal issues in environmental protection were therefore quite familiar to me, although without legal studies I was of course not specialized in them. But then I found a suitable subject. It had struck me that in Peru, despite relatively little effort for the environment, environmental protection at least has constitutional status, i.e. was explicitly mentioned in the constitution of the state. In Germany it was exactly the other way round, the various activities for the protection of the environment did not find any explicit support in the constitution. This contrast attracted me to some considerations on this subject, which I then put down on paper and, with the support of Martha from Konstanz, was able to translate into a useful Spanish.

However, I did not want to travel to South America just for the lecture, but on the way to Arequipa I wanted to get to know other countries as well. In search of cheap flights, I found an interesting and unbelievably cheap flight by Air France from Paris via Manaus/Brazil to Lima. Unfortunately, it was considerably more expensive as a forked flight, i.e. outward journey to Manaus and return journey from Lima, than for the outward and return flight to Lima. So, I decided to book Lima there and back, but then to get off in Manaus anyway. Of course, this was only possible without luggage, because otherwise the luggage would have automatically continued to Lima. Therefore, I could only travel with hand luggage. So did I and packed three shirts, one white, one good trousers, a jacket, some laundry, a travel iron and the most necessary washing stuff including a tube of textile detergent into a stable shopping bag and flew to Manaus, where I simply got off with my bag. The customs officer at the entry looked incredulously at my luggage: so few things, but an iron! He called a colleague, they both had a great time, but then they let me pass.

Manaus, today a big city with 2.2 million inhabitants, was still a lovely city in the 80s, well under 1 million inhabitants, in the middle of the Brazilian Amazon jungle. Founded in 1669 as a Portuguese fort at the strategically important mouth of the Rio Negro into the Amazon, which is still called Solimoes until then, and from 1791 the seat of the Portuguese governor, the city experienced an unprecedented boom between 1870 and 1910 as the world center of rubber production, which brought it great wealth. During this time, also the famous and gorgeous opera house was built, in which supposedly stars as Maria Callas appeared. Today, Manaus with its tropical, hot, and humid climate is still considered a tourist destination worth seeing, but also dangerous due to high crime rates.

Of course, I wanted to go out on the Amazonas occasionally, so I booked a day trip in an open boat together with some other tourists. We admired the confluence of the black Rio Negro coming from Venezuela with the yellow-brown Solimoes coming from Peru and the mile-long mixing of the different colors of these two rivers. We saw fantastic water lilies with leaves of almost 2 m diameter. And in the woods along the banks we could watch monkeys on the trees. We also visited an Indian village, probably mainly to be offered handicrafts. Towards the end of the boat trip I noticed that a somewhat younger couple was obviously amused about me. They spoke a strange German, which seemed Swiss to me. I spoke to them and was right, that is how I met Jörg and Elisabeth from Switzerland. The reason for their joy was my head, I had no headgear, and my already rather light hair offered no protection against the equatorial sun. So, I had got a veritable sunburn during the boat trip, which made my head appear in bright red. That must have looked funny, I got the receipt for the missing head protection the following night, when the sunburn started to hurt. But before that we went with the boat group to a pizzeria, and so we got to know each other better and exchanged our contact details. With Jörg, in the meantime with another partner, I am still good friends today.

From Manaus I went on to Brasilia, the official capital of the country. After landing at 3:00 a.m. I spent the rest of the night on a bench at the airport, the bag with my jacket and the good trousers for the lecture as a pillow, in order to have a look at the still quite newly built city the next morning. Apart from many modern functional buildings of the government there was not much to see, and the streets were almost deserted. On the same day I found another flight to Rio de Janeiro. At that time there was an Air-Pass in some countries, with which one could buy several domestic flights for a very reasonable total price. This allowed me to take several flights in Brazil.

Since I was in Rio de Janeiro several times later, I will report about this incredible city later. Same about Sao Paulo, my next stop. There I met a fellow student from my medical studies, Elisabeth, who was travelling around the area at the same time. We had compared our travel plans and had made a casual appointment in case we would be in Sao Paulo at the same time. Now we celebrated our meeting in the distance with a nice dinner and the next morning we travelled on together to Foz do Iguacu. From São Paulo there is a bus connection that covers the 1,050 km to Foz do Iguacu in just over 12 hours. But thanks to our Air-Passes we could afford a flight that only takes a good hour. The evening and the following day belonged to the fantastic Iguacu waterfalls. From my own comparisons with the Niagara Falls in the USA and the Victoria Falls in Africa, I consider the Iguacu Waterfalls to be the biggest and most beautiful in the world. The Rio Iguacu, which feeds the waterfalls, is a branch of the Rio Parana and represents the border between Brazil and Argentina. The waterfalls can be reached from both sides and can be viewed from different perspectives. From the open Brazilian side the whole width of the waterfalls can be seen, on the densely forested Argentinean side there are different viewpoints, among others a wooden footbridge to the Mirador Gargante del Diablo, the view into this "Devil's Throat", perhaps the most impressive part of the waterfalls. Buses take you on both sides to the border bridge over the river, which you can cross on foot. We spent the evening in the border town of Puerto Iguacu on the Argentine side of the river. The next morning, I said goodbye to Elisabeth, who wanted to return to Brazil, and flew from the small Argentinean airport near the city on to Buenos Aires.

For the Argentinean capital I had a perfect city guide, Julie, an Argentinean student who lived in downtown Buenos Aires and whom I had met some time ago in Düsseldorf. I called her and we met the next morning in front of the presidential palace, the Casa Rosada. We walked through the city together and she showed me the central Plaza de Mayor, the cathedral, the obelisk and some nice cafés, pubs, and restaurants. Although the country was in constant economic difficulties, the atmosphere on the streets that day was friendly and peaceful. After dinner, I took Julie to her parents' apartment and walked alone through the city at night to my hostel.

Now it was time for me to make my way towards Arequipa, as my lecture date was approaching. I noticed that flights from Buenos Aires to Lima were awfully expensive and finally found a much cheaper flight with Lloyd Aereo Boliviano (LAB) to La Paz/Bolivia. From there I went by bus to Lago Titicaca and then again took the Russian speedboat to Puno in Peru and further a bus to Juliaca. From there I wanted to take the train to Arequipa, but with the next scheduled train I would have arrived in Arequipa the day after next. As an alternative I could take a bus or the Collectivo. Collectivos are shared taxis that leave when they are full. I chose the collectivo because it was the cheapest and was already waiting. It might not have been the best idea. It took about two hours to fill the collectivo – complete! I was sitting in the front seat with another one on the right for the 6-hour drive on the 270 km to Arequipa. My bag with the jacket and the good trousers was somewhere in the trunk, luckily not on the roof. Because the in large parts unpaved road produced a lot of dust. Not only I was dusty when we finally arrived in Arequipa, but also my bag, however the dust got into the trunk. I found a cheap hotel near the Plaza de Armas, where the university building is located, and spent the next day doing the necessary cleaning, including ironing the white shirt and good pants with my specially carried travel iron. The next day at 06:00 p.m. the lecture should take place.

June 23rd, 1982 was the big day and the highlight of the trip. In the early afternoon I met Maria and Grace for a preliminary meeting. Since my Spanish skills were not sufficient for a discussion after the lecture, Grace agreed to help as a translator. Maria showed me a newspaper article that already reported about my arrival in Arequipa, even with a picture. Apparently, I had found good press officers with the two of them.

Shortly before 6:00 p.m. I arrived at the university in my now slightly wrinkled jacket, the freshly ironed shirt, the tie and the dusted and ironed good trousers. Before that, I had had my somewhat worn out shoes carefully cleaned by one of the numerous shoe cleaners in the Plaza de Armas. In the small assembly hall of the university, I found an expectant audience of students and some professors and was very warmly welcomed by the dean of the law faculty. After the presentation by the dean I could start with my lecture. It went quite well, and the audience listened quietly to my presentation. A slight smile on some faces was probably directed at the somewhat demolished gringo, who spoke in bumpy Spanish about German environmental law culture. My Spanish was later described by some students as "sweet and with a French accent". After friendly applause, the discussion started and there were indeed many questions. Grace and I bravely made it through this challenge and in the end, we were applauded again. In a smaller circle with the Dean and two other professors as well as Maria and Grace, we had a glass of champagne and a hearty thank you from the university. The two girls almost burst with pride.

The next morning Maria and I took the bus to Tacna to visit her parents. During the 6-hours bus ride over the 370 km distance there were dear kisses from my new friend, maybe out of gratitude for the successful presentation, which might have been useful for her university career. Or maybe as preparation for the visit, because, as I soon noticed, I was already considered by her parents as a possible son-in-law. Therefore, some kissing photos for the family album were urgently requested there as well.

Tacna is the southernmost city of Peru, about 30 km away from the border to Chile. The capital of the province of the same name has almost 100,000 inhabitants and is located at 550 m altitude on the Rio Caplina as an oasis in a stone desert landscape. Remarkable are the cathedral designed by Gustave Eiffel and the filigree stone arch Arco Parabolico which was built in front of it over the street.

Arriving in Tacna we were welcomed by Maria's siblings at the bus. I found a cheap hotel nearby and first I allowed myself a basic cleaning after the long drive over the dusty desert road. In the afternoon Maria picked me up and brought me to her home. The family - Maria's parents, Maria and her two sisters - lived in a beautiful house in the center of this charming little town. One of her sisters, Cecilia, even spoke English and was able to help me communicate. There was a nice dinner and a nice getting to know each other. However, it soon turned out that there was a crisis in the family. Only a short time later Maria's father left the family and soon after her mother moved with her three daughters to Arequipa.

For me, after the long round trip through South America, the time came for the return flight. I flew from Tacna directly to Lima and from there Air France brought me back home as planned with a stopover in Manaus and the change in Paris.

Unfortunately, I soon found out that my friendship with Maria was also very much seen from a material point of view. I received the news that her father, in financial difficulties, was unable to pay the installments of a loan and was therefore threatened with seizure and auction of the family home. I complied with her request for support and transferred an amount of DM 3,500 to Peru. After that, however, I heard nothing more about the further development of the problems or about a solution. And when Maria told me a little later that she had finally bought the video recorder she had wanted for a long time, I started to have some doubts. But I had no evidence for such a connection, and I suppressed the matter within me for the time being.

A few years later I finally fulfilled another wish of Maria and invited her to Düsseldorf. For her it was the first trip abroad. However, it also became apparent during this visit that she was mainly interested in material things and insignia of wealth. In her dreams she had expected a big car and a lot of domestic staff. But I did not have both, and her disappointment about this could not be overlooked. No domestic staff and a modest Peugeot 205 instead of the hoped-for Mercedes, this was not the equipment she had dreamed of for her guest accommodation. Nevertheless, we carried out my complete guest program, but our personal relationship remained friendly but distant during the three weeks. When we said goodbye at Frankfurt Airport, it was clear to both of us that our friendship probably had no future. On my next visit to Peru I ended the relationship explicitly.

Ancash - into the Cordillera Blanca

Once in Huaraz and having got the taste for it, the thought of the snow-covered peaks of the Cordillera Blanca never left me. I wanted to go there again, and deeper into the mountain world. The Cordillera Blanca are in total a national park, the Parque Nacional Huascaran. In this mountain range, the two highest mountains of Peru are right next to each other: The Nevado Huascaran, 6,768 m, is the highest mountain of Peru and the fourth highest mountain of South America. Three higher mountains are in the Argentinean Andes, the highest of which is the Aconcagua with 6,961 m. North of the Nevado Huascaran is the Huandoy, 6,360 m, the second highest mountain of the Cordillera Blanca. Between these two mountains lies the valley Quebrada de Llanganuco with the two lakes Lagos Llanganuco at 3,850 m. A gravel road, the Ruta 106, leads up through the valley from the small village of Yungay (2,450 m), past Lagos Llanganuco and further over the Portachuelo Pass with an altitude of 4,767 m, finally towards the tropical east side of the mountain range.

During my research for another tour to Ancash, I had discovered a lodge near Lagos Llanganuco that offered accommodation and food and even made a quite comfortable impression. Such accommodations are exceedingly rare in this mountain world outside of Huaraz and so the Llanganuco Mountain Lodge, located at an altitude of 3,500 m, was chosen as the destination for the next trip. This trip should take place together with our son Abdon. I had invited him to accompany me to convey to him my enthusiasm for South America, but also to have the opportunity to talk to him in detail and in peace about his future. We had already made some journeys together, e.g. to the USA, and had had wonderful experiences. Abdon gladly accepted my offer and his girlfriend Charlie agreed. So, we both flew to Lima to start our adventure together.

Already the next morning at 7:00 o'clock it should continue to Cusco. So, we needed a cheap accommodation near the airport. I had found such a place during my preparation of the trip, the B&B de Kike, a clean hostel with very friendly owners, who also pick up and bring back their booked guests at the airport. If you wish, they also serve breakfast or even a small dinner, or at least a beer. Just the right thing.

Of course, the trip had to go to Cusco first, for Abdon, who visited Peru for the first time an absolute must! After the long flight to Lima, the late arrival around 8pm and the short night, getting up early at 4 a.m. to catch the flight to Cusco in time is no easy exercise. But we made it, and after a nice little breakfast the owner of the hostel took us to the airport.

We stayed in Cusco for a few days to experience the magic of this picturesque city with its great cultural past. Of course, excursions were also part of our program, especially the day trip to Machu Picchu. Another excursion led us to Sacsayhuaman, an old Inca fortress on the outskirts of Cusco and easily accessible by Collectivo. Sacsayhuaman was built in the 15th century. 20,000 men were needed to bring the many stone blocks, some of them weighing tons, from a quarry about 20 km away into the complex in 70 years and then to carve them in such a way that the individual stones of the walls lay seamlessly on top of each other without mortar. The largest of these stones is 9 m high, 5 m wide, 4 m thick and has a weight of 200 tons. It is hard to imagine how the workers managed to build these walls with the tools of the time. Sacsayhuaman was not only a fortress for the Incas, but probably also a sanctuary and a place for ceremonies. In the middle of the complex there is a mighty chair that was carved into a stone block, the so-called throne of the Inca.

A third excursion led to the sacred valley of the Incas, Valle Sagrado de los Inkas. Unfortunately, I had to make this already booked excursion alone, as Abdon had caught an intestinal infection and therefore had to spend the day in our simple but comfortable hotel. The excursion led first to the Sunday market in the small town Pisac, which I already knew from a previous trip. This earlier Sunday trip to Pisac was not done with the expensive tourist bus but much cheaper with a Collectivo. At a certain place in Cusco, there are cars available that take passengers to Pisac. The driver leaves as soon as the car is occupied to the last seat. This can sometimes take a while, there is no timetable. The cars are also in, let us say, quite different condition, so you should take a closer look, especially at the tires, and also have some luck. The Collectivos drive back again from a meeting point at the outskirts of Pisac.

The location of Pisac in the valley is photogenic, from the market a steep way leads partly over stairs through terraces on a mountain, where an old Inca fortress is located. The market itself has a tourist area, where the typical woven fabrics, ponchos, hats, sweaters, and all kinds of souvenirs are offered. Next to it is the - more interesting - part of the market where the locals buy their food, especially fruit and vegetables, as well as articles for household needs. At 10:00 a.m., the elders of the different tribes in their official costumes and with sticks as insignia of their dignity walk together to mass in the small church - an extremely popular photo motif with tourists. For a photo, the dignitaries are also happy to receive a good tip.

From Pisac, we continued our journey along the Urubamba River to Ollantaytambo, the last town in the Sacred Valley of the Incas. The city was a retreat of the Incas, when the Spaniards had taken the city of Cusco, it was obviously not discovered by the Spaniards. Thus, a part of the old town still consists of streets and buildings of the Incas, which survived the centuries relatively undamaged. At the edge of the city there is a big further Inca fortification with numerous temples and other buildings. In the middle of the fortress is the Temple of the Sun with a wall of six monoliths. On a hill opposite the fortress, halfway up, there are warehouses from the Inca period, so-called Pinkullyuna, in which grain supplies were stored dry and protected. Like Pisac, the town of Ollantaytambo is surrounded by terraced fields supported by walls.

We returned to Lima with a morning flight from Cusco and after an overnight stopover we went to a bus station with the destination Huaraz, the capital of the district Ancash. There are numerous bus companies operating this route. We decided to use the company Cruz del Sur for the 8-hour drive from Lima to Huaraz. This company is considered one of the safest in Peru and has consistently good ratings. The often double-decker buses look quite decent, even if the cleanliness of the interior could be improved. As the journeys are cheap, we allowed ourselves the luxury of the business class; these are a few reclining seats in the lower part of the bus and a small meal is also served. However, the additional comfort meant that Abdon largely slept through the interesting landscapes. From Lima, the route initially leads a good 200 km north on the Panamericana, except for a few smaller towns mostly through a sandy desert. The bus takes 3-4 hours for this part of the way, depending on the time of day. A turnoff then leads to the northeast, steadily upwards through a rather bare mountain landscape; only along the small river in the valley, through which the road leads, there is a rich and lush green vegetation. Some police controls must be passed on the way until the road finally reaches an altitude of 4,000 m. This high plateau is finally left again by another valley, in which at 3,000 m height Huaraz is located, altogether about 520 road kilometers away from Lima.

This time, however, the provincial capital Huaraz should only be a stopover on the way to the Cordillera Blanca. For acclimatization we stayed in the city for two days. For strenuous mountain hikes this is definitely not enough, at least one week of acclimatization is highly recommended. But longer hikes in the high altitude were also not our goal. A genuinely nice hotel for a relaxed stay is the Hotel Club Andino. From the room, one has a wonderful view over the city to some snow-covered peaks of the Cordillera Blanca. As the snow line in the Andes is at an altitude of approximately 5,000 m, one can easily imagine what kind of huge mountains they are. Surprised, we noticed that the owner of the hotel welcomed us in German, he is Swiss. Also, the cuisine of the quite good restaurant is recognizably Swiss. Our plan was to go from Huaraz by bus further along the valley 57 km to Yungay. From there the gravel road of the Ruta 106 goes uphill through the valley Quebrada de Llanganuco for 20 km in direction of Lagos Llanganuco, near which our planned accommodation is located. For this part of the route we should take a taxi. On the advice of our Swiss, we took a taxi directly from the hotel, this was, according to the advice, not much more expensive but much more reliable. The advice turned out to be reasonable, and so we reached our destination after a good 2 hours quite comfortably already.

The Llanganuco Mountain Lodge is located very lonely on an almost flat piece of land in the mountain landscape, 3,500 m high, close to a small lagoon. A young Englishman, Charlie Good, a mountain and sports enthusiast, has made his personal dream come true by building and running this lodge. Initially accompanied by only two big dogs, a woman joined him after the lodge was built, and in the meantime a child has joined them as well. The Lodge consists of two houses, in one of which Charlie lives with his family, and where the reception and a comfortable dining room are located. In another house, about 100 m away, there are several guest rooms of different sizes. The rooms are well and modern furnished and for the given conditions quite comfortable. Breakfast and dinner are offered, for lunch there is a packed snack available. Absolute highlights of this place are the location and the view. On one side the view goes deep down into the valley where the Huaraz highway runs. On the other side you have a direct view to the two snow-covered highest mountains of the Cordillera Blanca, which are situated next to each other - a dream! The breakfast at sunrise on the large terrace meadow of the lodge in the cool silence of this mountain world with this view was a great and unforgettable common experience for Abdon and me.

The afterwards planned footpath to the Lagos Llanganucos turned out to be too exhausting in the rising midday sun. We comfortably made it to the nearby border of the nature park, where a small entrance fee is to be paid. From there, there would have been some kilometers of dusty gravel road and a few hundred meters of altitude difference up to the lakes. But we found there a friendly car driver who was willing to take us to the lakes. Because of his penetrating and extraordinarily strong smell he remained in our permanent memory under the nickname "polecat". The Lagos Llanganuco are located in the valley Quebrada de Llanganuco exactly between the two highest mountains of the area, just below the snow line. We were able to enjoy this magnificent sight for a few hours before we found another car that took us back to the border of the nature park.

After two days we left our lodge and now we had a bigger stage ahead of us, which was unexpectedly long. The destination was Chiclayo for a visit with Teresa and her family. Therefore, we took a taxi down into the valley to Yungay. There, a bus, the Yungay-Express, was supposed to leave at about 10 a.m. for Chimbote at the Pacific coast, tickets for which are available in a shop in Yungay. So, we were in Yungay at 9 a.m. and after some searching and asking around I finally had the tickets in my hand. But at 10 o'clock there was no bus, we waited. The bus finally arrived at 10:30 a.m., a small minibus, our Yungay-Express. We found two window seats opposite in the bus, which was only half occupied at first. Later it became full.

Shortly before the next bigger town, Caraz, the bus left the main road 3N of Huaraz to follow a country road, Ruta 104. It leaves the valley to the west towards the Pacific coast and climbs first up to the Chicarhuapunta Pass at 4,314 m altitude. Then it goes downhill - but how! Part asphalt, part gravel road, a very narrow road, steep serpentines, many narrow tunnels, and some passages where it went up vertically on the left side of the road and down vertically on the right side. Abdon obviously did not feel well, he had never seen anything like that before, and he was mostly sitting on the side of the slope. After what felt like an endless descent under these road conditions, the bus stopped for half an hour at a simple restaurant. There were toilets and also a need to use them, but the incredibly penetrating stench made it impossible for me to relieve myself. I decided to move it to the bus station in Chimbote. This took longer than expected, but it worked!

Finally arriving at the bus station in Chimbote we realized that we would have to wait a few hours for the next direct bus to Chiclayo. However, we found a bus ready to leave for Trujillo. From Chimbote it is about 130 km north on the Panamericana to the next bigger city, Trujillo. From there to Chiclayo it is another 210 km in the same direction. So, there were still a good 5 hours bus ride ahead of us. As expected, we found an earlier bus to Chiclayo in the bus station of Trujillo. It became evening.

Around 21:00 o'clock we finally reached Chiclayo. Teresa, her husband Guido and her brother Gianfranco welcomed us very warmly at the bus station. By car we went to their house. There Teresa's sister, her mother and her daughter Melissa welcomed us. We were treated with great Peruvian hospitality. There was a big dinner and a lot to tell. Gianfranco had cleared his room for us and had moved in with his sister Melissa. The next day we celebrated Teresa's birthday together. There was a lot of food, there was singing and, in the evening, Melissa performed some dances from Peruvian folklore in appropriate costumes. Among other things, she danced the Marinera, a Peruvian national dance that originated on the north coast in the Chiclayo region, together with her father. The dancer is courted by her partner in three-four time with brass music, both wave white handkerchiefs and support the rhythm with castanets. The next day we spent on the beach in the small village of Pimentel, just 12 km from Chiclayo. In a very simple restaurant on the beach we had, among other things, ceviche, my favorite Peruvian dish made of marinated raw fish - a dish that should not be eaten in such a simple restaurant, which I should have known.

For the return trip to Lima we saved ourselves the 14-hour bus trip for the almost 800 km on the Panamericana to the south and chose the one-and-a-half-hour flight that same evening. A good decision, because as punishment for my reckless favorite dish on the beach, I got a regular diarrhea, which lasted for the next day. So, Abdon had to spend our last day in Lima alone while I guarded the hotel room. For the return flight I was fit again.

Peru photo tour and a failed pass crossing

After the good experiences of my trip with Abdon - he once said it was the most beautiful trip of his life - six years later I had the opportunity again to invite a guest to a trip to Peru to show him the beauty of this country and especially of the Ancash region. It was my old friend Peter, who had once conveyed a very good job for me many years before and thus changed my life forever. Here was the opportunity for a revenge. Peter has a small marketing company which was not doing very well at that time and he is also a professional photographer. The prospect of fantastic photo opportunities in Peru filled us both with great anticipation.

64

For the journey to Lima we treated ourselves to the comfortable KLM Business Class, which considerably increased the travel pleasure right from the beginning of the trip. And again, the first overnight stay took place in the friendly B&B de Kike, where I was immediately recognized and greeted joyfully. Early the next morning we went to Cusco, where we completed the well-proven excursion program. In Cusco, on Machu Picchu and in Pisac, Peter took the first wonderful photos, which were later published in a beautiful illustrated book. From Machu Picchu, he even managed to climb Huayna Picchu, the sugar loaf-shaped elevation high above the holy city - quite an effort at this altitude, which I did not expect myself to make.

The stay in Cusco, however, was unusually comfortable. As I was able to accumulate bonus points in the meantime due to many professional trips with some hotel chains, I was able to accommodate us in Cusco for three days in the noble hostel Palacio del Inka with the support of these points, which we enjoyed very much.

Then we went on to the jungle of the Amazon region with a flight to Puerto Maldonado. From the former - and probably still current - gold mining town on the Rio Madre de Dios we went by bus and boat on a tributary, the Rio Tambopata, to the Reserva Nacional Tambopata region to the Posada Amazonas Lodge. This lodge offered the opportunity for daily excursions by boat or on foot into the jungle to admire the magnificent rainforest and observe animals - and this at a relatively comfortable level. The huts for two people were open to one side to allow the guests to experience the closeness to nature. This proximity to the creatures of the jungle is not for anxious minds. The variety of noises in the jungle is sometimes irritating. So, the first night we puzzled over a sound that resembled the engine noise of an old Ju52 airplane. The next morning, we asked one of the rangers and it turned out that howler monkeys make these sounds. An equally open dining room, a bar and a large lounge with hammocks as well as proper sanitary facilities rounded off the facilities. The water was filtered directly from the river, drinking water was available in carafes from the canister. Electricity came from a generator from 18:00 to 22:00, also the time for charging the smartphones. Even a weak WiFi was available during this time. The rubber boots that were put on daily for the hikes were part of the basic equipment for the often-muddy paths through the jungle. It had been raining a lot lately, and so the water on the narrow paths was sometimes so high that it threatened to run into the boots when wading through. A hike led to a metal lookout tower that still overlooked the tops of the trees, allowing a wonderful view over the dense green of the jungle. However, the steps of the spiral staircase were made of metal grids, so that the damp clay from the boots was loosened through the grids and trickled down - a real disadvantage for the last in the line of climbers. Besides monkeys and numerous bird species, mosquitoes were our constant companions and required appropriate countermeasures. We spent the short evenings up to the "black-out" in funny company with other travelers at the bar, which among other things produced a very tasty Pisco sour - the Peruvian national drink with addictive potential!

After three days our jungle time was up, and we went back to Puerto Maldonado and from there by flight via Cusco to Lima for an overnight stay. The next morning, we took off early to the airport for a car rental. Because this time I wanted to explore the mountain region Ancash by car myself. We got an upgrade for a nice off-road vehicle and drove comfortably through the morning rush hour traffic from Lima towards Huaraz. I knew the route, and Peter also had a powerful GPS device and gave the navigator. But we wanted to go further on to reach the Llanganuco Mountain Lodge the same day. So, we went from Huaraz first on the main road to Yungay and then turned right and uphill towards the lodge. But here, on the variety of small and smallest gravel and grass tracks, my memory somehow reached its limits after six years, as well as the GPS device. We became insecure and when we reached a very dilapidated wooden bridge that seemed to be completely unknown to me, we wondered if it could really carry our jeep. She made it and we kept on driving uphill because it could not be that wrong. After some searching and back and forth, we finally found our lodge - and that was a good thing, because it was getting dusky in the meantime.

Again, I was fascinated by the unbelievable situation of this lodge and its calmness in the middle of the huge mountain world, and Peter was also extremely impressed. It got dark very quickly now, and we retreated to the dining room for dinner and a first exchange of ideas with the founder of the lodge, Charlie Good. On the way back to our room we experienced a fantastic starry sky in the clear mountain air, which was not covered by any clouds or air pollution. The night in the comfortable room and the surrounding silence was relaxing after the long drive. The next morning, I could experience once again, this time with Peter, the highlight of this location, the breakfast at sunrise in the clear cold air on the terrace meadow of the lodge. It was Peter's birthday. First the snow-covered mountain peaks shone in white light while the valley was still in darkness, then the light line moved rapidly downwards until we too sat in the sunlight with our hot coffee in our hands. We enjoyed the wonderful atmosphere of this place and discussed our plan for the day: to drive into the national park to the Lagos Llanganucos, and then further over the adventurously narrow and steep pass road up to the height of 4.767m of the Portachuelo Pass. Unfortunately, we started quite late and the penalty followed on foot. An oncoming and rather fast car threw a stone which damaged the windshield of our car. Nevertheless, we drove on to the Lagos Llanganucos, where Peter found fantastic photo motives with which lakes between the enormous snow mountains, so that we stayed in this area for a longer time. In the meantime, time had also progressed, so that we were worried about the ascent and descent on the pass road before dusk. In addition, we were worried whether the banged-up windshield would still survive the ride on the bumpy track. So after only three of the numerous hairpins we decided with a heavy heart not to take the rest of the pass road. But at that moment it was clear to me that this could not be the last word - and indeed this story was continued a few years later. But now, the next morning, we went back to Lima.

In Lima I had already discovered the Hotel Fourpoints in the district of Miraflores in earlier years, which was reasonably priced in a particularly good location in the city. In addition, I could use my bonus points collected at Starwood in this hotel to reduce the price. Miraflores is one of the posh business districts in Lima, located directly at the Pacific Ocean, with good shops and nice restaurants. Here you can also eat my favorite dish Ceviche without hesitation, which I have done regularly.

In Miraflores I had made an appointment with Teresa, who was staying with relatives in La Molina, a distant wealthy suburb of Lima. At 10:00 a.m. we were to meet in the lobby of our hotel. Teresa did not arrive; she was still out and about. After several mails back and forth we finally met shortly before 12:00 p.m. in Larcomar, a beautiful viewpoint on the Pacific coast, not far from our hotel. Peter reacted a little angry about this delay, maybe without knowing that the trip from La Molina to Miraflores takes about 2 hours and that the bus connection is not always reliable and on time. Peter was also irritated about my familiarity with Teresa. Thus, the common day stood from the outset under an unfavorable star. We drove together to the old town of Lima, where Peter looked for photo motives, while I had a lot to talk about with Teresa. The situation became even more tense when Melissa, Teresa's daughter, spontaneously joined us. The two women had a lot talking together, and somehow, they did not find a common wavelength with Peter - obviously, there was no real sympathy. I finally defused the increasingly conflict-laden situation by actively ending their being together, which caused me some problems with my old friend Teresa and her daughter afterwards. The "sending away" is hardly acceptable for a Peruvian woman, and Melissa probably never really forgave me for it either. But after all, this was also the last evening of my trip with Peter, for which I had made a considerable effort and which I absolutely wanted to bring to a harmonious end. This was successful, the end of the day in a nice street restaurant near our hotel at Ceviche and Pisco sour was peaceful. The next day I met Teresa alone again, there were tears, apologies and finally the reconciliation hoped for by both sides. The problems of the day before were thus cleared up for me on both sides. The unhappy day was forgotten, Peter and I could finish our trip with the flight home starting in the evening in the comfortable KLM Business Class. Later I received a nice photo book with Peter's photos as a thank you for the invitation.

Once again Ancash - a question of honor

The failure of the broken off pass trip into the magnificent mountain landscape above the Lagos Llanganucos continued to gnaw inside me. Until, after a few years, I decided to make up for this missed highlight of my experiences in the beautiful province of Ancash in a week trip to Peru. The plan was to fly to Lima, rent a car and cross the Portachuelo Pass after a stopover in the provincial capital Huaraz, spend two nights in a lodge and then return to Lima with a stopover in Huaraz. A last overnight stay in Lima should then complete the weekly program. I could not find a fellow traveler for this somewhat crazy plan - and to be honest, I did not really want to. It was my personal confrontation with the defeat that I had not yet managed to achieve this small triumph in my travel plans.

But my plan was not without problems. The Ruta 106, which leads past the Lagos Llanganuco to the pass, is not one of the ten most dangerous roads in the world, but it is anything but easy. A partly quite loose gravel road, which narrows considerably after passing the lakes and mostly offers space for only one vehicle with rather rare places to avoid, steep slopes without securing at the roadside and finally felt endless narrow and steep serpentines lead high up to almost the snow line of 5,000 m height. In addition, there is traffic, also small trucks and minibuses occasionally drive on this stretch. In dry weather all this is possible, but there are also occasional continuous rainfalls in this area, most of the times connected with landslides, which make these small roads extremely dangerous. Since I had to book the trip early for cost reasons, I also needed a plan B and C in case of unsuitable weather conditions, that could make the passage via Ruta 106 impossible or too dangerous. But even for this case, attractive alternative destinations were quickly found.

After all, the idea of doing this tour alone required some thought and planning, and by no means met with undivided enthusiasm from family and friends. A mental analysis of possible scenarios showed me that in most cases the risks in pairs were hardly less than alone. And even if I considered these residual risks to be rather small after careful planning, I did not like to unnecessarily involve another person. So, the previous plan A was retained, supplemented by the bad weather alternatives B and C. Everything is better than doing nothing and staying in the routine, says Paulo Coelho:

"Si piensas que la aventura es peligrosa, prueba la rutina. Es mortal."
("If you think the adventure is dangerous, try the routine... ...it's deadly.")

There was still the search for a suitable accommodation, preferably on the other side of the pass, as I wanted to cross it. And indeed, I found one single lodge, the Andes Lodge Peru, in the small village of Yanama, on Ruta 106 about 25km behind the pass. This was the chance to enjoy the up and downhill on both sides of the pass.

The journey to Lima was once again by KLM via Amsterdam. A - as usual - very friendly purser walked through the rows and talked to the passengers. My seat neighbor, a banker from Israel, told him that he only wanted to stay in Lima for one day for a conference, so it was to go back to Israel the very next day. The purser was amazed and then asked me about my destinations. I said that I wanted to stay for a whole week.
"Is it going to Cusco and Machu Picchu?" he asked.
"No, I've been there before," I said. And then I explained my goal to him: To go by car up a mountain pass road and down the other side, and then after two overnight stays, the same thing again in the other di-

rection. And once again the purser was amazed: *"That's why you're flying to Peru now? I've never heard anything like it!"*
And still thinking about the two lunatics in row 2, he went on to the next row.

The owners of the B&B de Kike had become dear acquaintances to me in the meantime, and the welcome at the airport and in the house was accordingly warm. The usual room was reserved for me, as well as a small snack, a big beer, and a nice conversation. After breakfast the next morning, they took me to the airport where I rented my car, a small SUV with petrol engine and manual gear shift. Then I started in the direction of Huaraz. The first hurdle with the strange car comes already at the airport of Lima right at the beginning: Turning into the main road at a big roundabout with several lanes which you have to cross directly to get into the right direction, namely north. Once this is done, it gets much more relaxed. In Lima, people do not drive very aggressively, but they like to drive a little bit crisscross. The Peruvians also make three or four lanes out of two, which creates a certain mixture when you thread it back in. Generally overtaking is a kind of popular sport, the tighter it gets the more heroic. And one quickly learns that keeping to speed-limits is annoying and leads to even more daring overtaking maneuvers by the following cars. But there are also radar controls, especially on the northern arterial roads of Lima.

The way to Huaraz was still in my memory after the last trips to this area, and so I reached the Hotel Club Andino again in the afternoon with the friendly Swiss owner and the beautiful view to the snow-covered mountains of the Cordillera Blanca. A quiet evening in the restaurant and in my room gave me the opportunity to prepare once again for the pass trip the next day.

Early in the morning I started with a packed lunch, first on the federal road 3N to Yungay and then on the gravel road of the Ruta 106 towards Lagos Llanganucos. The weather was fantastic and ideal for my tour, already since my arrival in Lima. The alternative plans B and C had long since disappeared in a lower corner of my travel bag. The snow mountains gave a strong contrast to the blue sky and the landscape showed its most beautiful structure in the morning sun. A stay in the beautiful Llanganuco Mountain Lodge was not planned this time, so I followed the 106 directly to the two lakes. Near to the second lake, there was the opportunity for a break and a first grab into a packed lunch, the whole thing with the wonderful view to the lakes and the mountain world. Even here, from a height of almost 4,000 m, the further ascending pass road still looked quite steep and high.

And then the Portachuelo Pass project could begin. The engine hummed well, and the car pushed itself slowly up the shaky gravel road in first gear, always careful not to get too close to the side of the road on the slope. First gear remained the standard for the rest of the journey. With the first of the steep serpentines came the habituation and an increasing feeling of safety. Now it was important to notice in time if another vehicle was approaching. So, the view went not only forward on the road, but always a few serpentines further up, to recognize another vehicle or at least its dust cloud in time. Then it was necessary to quickly find one of the few passing points and wait there for the passage of the other vehicle. If the passing point was on the downhill side, this provided a small additional adrenaline rush and a particularly careful shunting maneuver. And not always such a passing place was found. In case of doubt, the agile vehicle must back off. An oncoming small truck brought me into this situation, but fortunately it was only about 100 m. In a later situation, even a minibus kindly put me back a bit to let me pass. The drivers of these minibuses are true artists. Halfway up, a lookout point gave a welcome opportunity for a short break and some photos of the lakes and the mountain scenery. In the further course the Ruta 106 became a little bit narrower and the gravel even looser, so that full concentration was necessary. Finally, only a few serpentines above me were recognizable and then finally I reached a small parking place for a few cars, behind which a gap in the rock cleared the way to the other side of the pass.

The pass height of 4,767 m was reached. And thus a unique view, from just below the snow line down into the valley and at the same time still high up to the two highest peaks of the Cordillera Blanca - and all this in the beginning midday sun with a bright blue sky. The silence, only occasionally interrupted by a passing vehicle, made the enormous nature seem even more impressive. The plan had succeeded, I had reached my goal. I stayed at this place for quite a while to absorb and enjoy the view and the atmosphere. I only felt the altitude when I, to escape from the view of the road for a moment, followed a path that rose a little further.

Already after a few meters of altitude the air became scarce and I had to stop again.

Then I went on downhill on the other side towards Yanama. The track on this side of the pass was altogether much better and easier than on the Llanganuco side. Nevertheless, there was a moment of shock when suddenly and unexpectedly a stone, about the size of a grapefruit, hit the road about 10 m in front of my car. Fortunately, the emerging fear that more stones might follow was unfounded. Later I learned that rock falls of this kind were a major risk on this road. In Yanama, although only a small mountain village, I had to search and ask a little bit to find the Andes Lodge Peru. There are no hints or signs to the lodge. Finally arrived I was directed through a gate into the garden to a meadow for parking.

The Andes Lodge Peru is a small family business of father, mother, and daughter. The father is responsible for house and garden, the mother for kitchen, reception and accounting and the daughter, at that time still studying tourism, for marketing and e-mail in English. For cleaning and room service there is a temp. The lodge with its three rooms is quite inexpensive, breakfast and dinner are included. The rooms are quite simple but clean; the most beautiful room is a corner room with big windows and a double bed. I had a smaller room with two narrow single beds. One must know that in the mountains it can get very cold at night, and the lodge is still located at an altitude of 3,400 m. The rooms are unheated, the floor is very cold, and the duvets are rather light too. So, I quickly learned to use the blanket from the second bed in addition and not to take off my socks at night. For the meals, there are two dining tables in the living room of the family that also serves as a lounge for the guests. The atmosphere is cozy, the portions are plentiful and consist especially of the variety of Peruvian potatoes. The delicious Cuscena beer was available right away in the liter bottle. On the first evening I was alone with the family, on the second day I was joined by a Brazilian group of four people and three SUVs, who had already made the long way from Rio de Janeiro through Amazonia and now wanted to continue over the pass to Huaraz and Lima. We had fun and good entertainment together in our language diversity.

The next morning, early at 7:00 a.m., I started on my way back to Huaraz, back into the mountains and up to the Portachuelo pass. So, the same route back - and yet it was completely different! While on the way there the mountains shone in the light of the midday sun, they now showed themselves in the warm light of the sunrise with long shadows, seemingly a completely different landscape than before. The shadows made the mountains seem even more powerful than in bright daylight. The ascent was uncomplicated, and I was looking forward to enjoying the wonderful view from the top of the pass again. A little bit proud of having made it this far, I experienced quite a disillusionment at the pass summit. On the parking lot a young Peruvian cyclist stood with his mountain bike and grinned at me friendly. He does not even look particularly exhausted. Okay, there I stood with my performance of driving an SUV up the mountain, and this boy had mastered the same difficult road with its entire ascent on a mountain bike! Probably not the first time either, as our following conversation revealed. I could only congratulate him on this achievement. While I stayed at this impressive place for a while, he made his way back. Some men in working clothes were also in the parking lot, they were, as I learned, responsible for detecting loose boulders to prevent rockfall and to remove stones from the roadway.

Then I went down again, slowly, and carefully over the loose gravel and steep serpentines, past the beautiful lakes and through the long valley down to Yungay. There I finally reached the Plaza de Armas, where I found a parking place and took a deep breath. The adventure was over, and the upcoming drive to Huaraz and Lima was nothing more but a piece of cake. I looked at my hands and felt that despite all the joy about the successful project I had more adrenalin in my blood than I thought. So, I took a half hour break on a park bench on the plaza. Back at the parking place I noticed how much the car was looking at the long drive over the dusty road inside and outside, it was totally dirty up to all joints and cracks. So, I stopped at the next gas station and asked for a car wash. A boy offered to do it and then went to work with hose, bucket, rag and leather. It took him an hour and a half to do the job, which was a good opportunity for me to get some rest. In the end, the car shone in its most beautiful glow wherever you looked. The price demanded was ridiculously low, I gave him double after extensive praise for his good work.

Back in Huaraz in the Club Andino there was the opportunity to relax in the well heated room and restaurant with a good wine and a last view to the snow-covered mountains of the Cordillera Blanca in the evening sun. The next day followed the comfortable 8-hours-drive back to Lima with small breaks and the return of the rental car at the airport. But I wanted to stay one more day in Lima and so I took the airport bus to Miraflores to the Hilton Hotel near my Fourpoints Hotel.

The next day I had a lunch date with Teresa, she came by plane from Chiclayo and with the same bus from the airport as I did the evening before, so we also met in front of the Hilton. For a while we sat in a café at Larcomar, I told her about my trip to the mountains and she was happy about my feelings for the beauty of her country. We looked at the Pacific Ocean, the surfers on their waves and the motorized paragliders flying along the coast and enjoyed our reunion. Then we walked up Avenida Jose Larco to Parque John F. Kennedy, where there are some nice street restaurants. A portion of Ceviche, a Pisco sour and an espresso rounded off our afternoon together. Teresa left for La Molina to visit her relatives and I went to my hotel and from there by taxi to the airport. At 08:00 p.m. the KLM started again in direction Amsterdam.

Other destinations in Latin America

Mexico and Guatemala

My first trip to Latin America, at the same time my first long-distance trip and, at the age of 23, my first ever flight, took me to Mexico together with my first wife Brigitte. It was a one-week package tour, a special offer from a smaller tour operator. The plane, a Boeing 707 of Condor, was quite old, and the flight was quite bumpy in places. We sat far in the back and I got a window seat on the right, because Brigitte was already more experienced in flying. So, I had a good view of the landscape, but also of the right wing and the two engines attached to it. And when the first heavy turbulences came up over the Atlantic, I found the sight of the wing quite irritating. I did not know yet how far the wings can bend in turbulence. And the engines too seemed to lead a life of their own with their vibrations. I remembered some of the lectures from my engineering studies, especially those in engineering mechanics, which had dealt with material fatigue and fracture behavior. Brigitte was asleep, apparently, she was familiar with the feeling in a wobbling aircraft in turbulence. Even when a dream-like sunset loomed over the Atlantic, she was not inclined to interrupt her sleep for it. I asked the stewardess for a mini bottle of wine and enjoyed this beautiful sight alone.

Mexico City was already a huge city, a juggernaut with many millions of inhabitants. Official censuses reflect only a part of the actual number of inhabitants, which is realistically estimated at over 20 million today. Even the seemingly endless approach over the sea of houses to the international airport gives an idea of the sheer size of the city. Some parts of the city are well developed for tourism and are regarded as reasonably safe, while others are considered dangerous. The city was founded in the 14th century by the Aztecs under the name Tenochtitlan on an island in a big lake and was destroyed by the Spaniards in the year 1521. Only one year later, the reconstruction of the city began at the same place under the name Ciudad de Mexico (Mexico City). The location on the former lake is still a problem for the city today, many of the magnificent and very heavy buildings, such as the Angel de la Independencia or the magnificent Palacio de Bellas Artes, have already sunk considerably into the muddy subsoil.

In the one week of the guided tour, one could really only experience the most important of the countless sightseeings of Mexico City, the Palacio Nacional, the big colonial style cathedral at the Zocalo, the Plaza de la Constitucion, the huge Chapultepec-Park, the famous Museo Nacional de Antropologia and the canals of Xochimilco that give an idea that the city was originally built on a lake. Especially there, but also almost everywhere else, there are mariachi chapels and street food in the streets. Once I could not resist the delicious sight and the next day, I regretted it bitterly. "Peel it, boil it, cook it or forget it" is the rule that you should always keep in mind even in Mexico. On the other hand, a special experience was a dinner in the restaurant on the 44th floor of the Torre Latinoamericana, the highest building in the city built in 1956 on 361 piles, with a fantastic view over the sea of houses in Mexico City.

A little later there was a second flight with Brigitte to Mexico City and from there a guided tour over the Yucatan Peninsula and then through Guatemala to Honduras. Destination of the trip were different buildings from the Maya culture, like Chichen-Itza, Uxmal, Palenque and Tikal. But also, the passage through Guatemala with the historical capital Antigua, the beautifully situated Atitlan mountain lake, and the mystical Indian market of Chichicastenango brought many impressive experiences. Guatemala is well known for its volcanoes and numerous earthquakes as well as for beautiful colorful weavings, which also play an important role in the clothing of the population. On the long bus trip to Honduras and the Mayan city of Tikal, there was a scandal. When Brigitte urgently asked for a toilet and, as none was accessible, would have been satisfied with a bush by the roadside, the tour guide strictly refused on moral grounds. The dispute dragged on, but despite loud protests also from other tour participants, she and the bus driver consistently refused to stop the bus. An agonizing hour of further waiting time was the result, until we reached the destination Tikal and the longed-for relief could take place. The tour guide, who was severely insulted by me and several other participants, fled into the bus crying, while the group was guided through the fantastic Mayan city by a local guide.

We did not return to the bus. I had discovered a small landing strip next to the plant and approached a pilot who was standing there next to his small twin-engine aircraft. He agreed to fly Brigitte and me back to Guatemala City at a fair price, from where our return flight to Mexico City was scheduled for the next day. The border and customs formalities were quickly completed by our local pilot. We briefly informed one of our fellow travelers about our disappearance and flew off, while the rest of the group prepared for the long bus ride back to Guatemala City. On the way the pilot told us about his life, and so we learned that the comfortably furnished plane was a private plane of former US President Lyndon B. Johnson, which had somehow finally arrived in Guatemala on adventurous ways. Arrived in Guatemala City, we spent the rest of this exciting day comfortably in our booked hotel.

Many years later, I came again with Cecilia, my father and stepmother on a similar trip through Mexico. Even later I wanted to go to Guatemala again and took a Spanish course in Antigua for one week alone. Eight hours daily of private lessons are unbelievably cheap there, so that even compared to a course in Spain the long journey is worth it. My teacher shared my opinion that textbooks are rather boring and so the lessons consisted of us taking turns telling each other about our lives in the form of interviews. Gross mistakes were corrected immediately and in between there was a little grammar and fine-tuning. So, we had a great time together and laughed a lot during the lessons. The daily eight hours were never boring and the exploration of the historical capital Antigua and one of the very frequent small earthquakes there made for an interesting and exciting week.

Venezuela

My first contact with Venezuela was on my honey-moon with Cecilia. We had spontaneously taken advantage of a special offer from our Düsseldorf airline LTU, which had newly included the route to Venezuela from Düsseldorf via Porlamar on the Isla de Margarita to Barcelona/Venezuela in its program. For this purpose, we booked a one-week round trip, among others to the Canaima Nature Park. Group trips in the bus are not really my thing, the daily quiet or even loud scramble for the best seats in the bus and the often-requested toilet and cigarette breaks are rather annoying. But we had an excellent and very likeable local travel guide, Carlos. And we met Hartmut and his girlfriend at the time Brigitte on the trip. With Hartmut, also an engineer, I immediately found a good basis for conversation and so we spent our trip in nice company. Later Hartmut accompanied us on our second trip to Mexico with my father and my step-mother. Even though we only rarely meet each other since then, Hartmut and his wife Sakura are still among our good and very esteemed friends.

From the coastal city of Barcelona, we went by bus to Ciudad Bolivar on the Orinoco. One of the only two bridges over the Orinoco river connects the capital of the state of Bolivar with the northern parts of the country. There is an airport too, from which we arrived with small airplanes to the nature park Canaima in the south. After some tours and hikes in this beautiful environment we had the opportunity to fly again with a small Cessna to the waterfall Salto Angel, which is with about 1km height surely one of the highest waterfalls in the world. Cecilia voluntarily sat down on a single seat at the very back of the plane and with only little visibility. We landed on a small runway near the waterfall, visited an Indian village and watched the waterfall from a distance. There was not that much to see because we couldn't get any closer and the waterfall had very little water this season. Also, from the plane, with which our pilot Hannibal tried to fly close to the Table Mountain, the visibility was not much better with low hanging clouds. Hannibal flew some fast turns on the way back to avoid the cloud towers and Cecilia had to throw up.

The flight back to Ciudad Bolivar and the drive to Barcelona were unspectacular except for one member of the group, a high school teacher, who often and gladly spoke loudly with his video camera to comment on his pictures and thus alternately annoyed and amused all of us. At the last dinner of the tour group I said goodbye to Carlos with a little table talk, during which I also tried some Spanish sentences about the beauty of the country and the kindness of the inhabitants. At the concluding *"Viva la Venezuela!"* strangers also stood up at the neighboring tables and clapped their hands.

As a result, the feeling remained in me that we had made a nice honeymoon trip to Venezuela, but that we had only got a very fleeting impression of the beauty of this country during this group trip. Also, the Salto Angel is mostly described as a mighty and impressive waterfall, and that did not correspond at all to our experience. We had obviously just been there at the wrong time. So, we had to start a new trip, and this time it was definitely an individual trip. Until then, however, it should still take many years. But the plan matured and from a lot of research about the country and possible travel routes, a new travel plan on an individual basis was finally created, in which also modules of local travel providers were integrated. These also included overnight stays in tents and hammocks, and that was the point when Cecilia said goodbye to these travel plans. So, I should and wanted to travel alone again.

On a Sunday morning in July I started with the rainproof jacket and the tried and tested shoulder bag. This time with Lufthansa, via Frankfurt to Caracas and from there after a five-hour wait with a regional airline to Puerto Ordaz (Ciudad Guyana) at the Orinoco river. An airport shuttle brought me to the Hotel Eurobuilding Guayana in the late evening. A good hotel, and that was a good thing, because I was tired and wanted to start early the next morning to escape the midday heat. Besides, I still had no idea from where and with which bus it should go on to Ciudad Bolivar. So, I had to ask my way through, and I succeeded, and a little later I was sitting in a comfortable long-distance bus in the right direction. It was clearly more difficult to find my hotel with the nice name Posada Casa Grande de Angostura, as for security reasons there was no reference to a hotel at the given address. A friendly taxi driver helped me and rang the bell at different doors until he finally found out which door was the right one. But there, nobody answered our ringing. I thanked the helpful driver and decided to wait. After a good hour it was time, my ringing was heard, and the door was opened. The problem of the last hour was only that I had not thought of the lunch siesta that is usual here. From the roof terrace of the hotel I enjoyed the view over the Orinoco to a black cloud wall, which slowly approached and indicated a thunderstorm with many lightnings, until the heavy rain drove me away from the roof terrace.

In the early morning of the next day I took the Cessna again to Canaima. On a boat trip I met a shaman from a neighboring tribe, and we started talking about the therapeutic possibilities of different plants from the jungle. He also told me about a little girl with a burn on her leg, which he had been treating for some time but without much success and asked me to have a look at the girl. We then walked - already at dusk - across swampy meadows and through the forest to a hut where a family had gathered around the bench where the girl was lying. She had a round, perhaps 6 cm large and inflamed burn on her left leg but was otherwise in good condition. The family did not consider a performance in a surgical outpatient clinic, as the girl would have had to fly to Ciudad Bolivar. Fortunately, there was reasonably clean water to clean my hands and the area around the wound. I dressed the wound with disinfecting Betaisadona ointment and - as good as possible - a sterile bandage and gave the shaman the rest of the tube of ointment, some sterile compresses, and a pack of antibiotics with instructions. I was not happy only with this temporary therapy, but maybe the shaman's joint appearance with the bearded gringo and the miracle ointment had a healing psychological effect too. On the way back in the darkness I was glad to have the shaman with me as a local guide.

The next morning a small travel group started early in the morning with a boat upstream. We were accompanied by two locals, the guide, again a shaman, and the boat driver at the outboard motor. This time the Salto Angel should be explored by water. It had rained a lot lately and the river had enough water. However, there were also numerous rapids, which required a lot of skill and probably a lot of experience from the boat driver. After turning into a side river, the rapids increased, sometimes so much that the motor could hardly manage to cope with them. The boat lurched heavily in the force of the water masses, and not all the small group could really enjoy the adventure. Finally, we reached our destination, our overnight stay, in the middle of the forest and directly at the river. There were tables and benches, a rack with hammocks and some toilets and showers.

To get from there to the viewpoint on the Salto Angel there was another mountain to climb. It rained a little bit and the way up was steep, actually not a path at all, but a network of thick roots, over which you had to climb, always being careful not to slip on the damp smooth woods. As the eldest of the group I was slower than the others, so I let them go ahead, to determine my own safe pace in peace. Finally arrived, from half height, a magnificent view opened up on the full circumference of the mighty waterfall, which this time also carried plenty of water. The rain had subsided, and we all let this wonderful sight sink in silence. The further way, down to the foot of the waterfall, was closed because of the current unusually large amount of water in the river. After an hour at this beautiful place I decided to start the way back on my own at my own pace. An Australian tourist, Sue, offered me to come along so that I would not have to walk alone. I gratefully accepted the offer and so we both set off on the slippery and quite strenuous way down. Back at camp I dropped onto the next chair, sweaty and exhausted. But only a few deep breaths later Sue suddenly stood in front of me again, stark naked, and said she wanted to take a shower now. And do I want to come with her. A pretty sight, I admit. And I, too, felt like a shower, but not more. So, I thanked her for the friendly offer and let her go into the shower alone.

The twilight is short in this area, it gets dark quickly. The dinner out of the big picnic boxes with candlelight and some mosquitoes was atmospheric and a nice community experience. Even Sue did not hold my cancellation against me, and we still laughed a lot that evening. My first night in a hammock in the middle of the forest was not as uncomfortable as I had feared. I slept well.

The return trip by boat the next morning went much faster through the rapids with the current than the day before. Back in Canaima and with the Cessna to Ciudad Bolivar to my posada, I took the bus again the next morning to Puerto Ordaz, from where my next tour should start - into the jungle of the Orinoco Delta.

In fact, my driver was waiting for me at the reception of the Hotel Eurobuilding Guayana at 7:00 am on time to pick me up and bring me to Tucupita. To my surprise I was the only passenger. For the route, the Orinoco had to be crossed first. So, I also got to know the second bridge over this river, there are no more bridges. Tucupita, a small city of nearly 100.000 inhabitants at the Rio Manamo, the most northern of the many arms of the Orinoco Delta, is located at the edge of the large jungle area in the interior of the Delta. The road ends here, there is a small airfield, otherwise it is only possible to continue by boat. So, I said goodbye to my driver here and was already expected in the small harbor. After two and a half hours of driving I went 2 hours downstream in the boat towards my booked jungle camp. Also, in the boat I was the only guest, but together with a lot of freight, obviously to supply the camp. To my delight I discovered some boxes with delicious looking fruit underneath. Shortly after leaving the city there was only dense seemingly impenetrable forest on both sides of the river. The camp consisted of a large wooden building for the common rooms and individual huts for the accommodation of the guests. The wooden huts were open to the river, inside there was a basket for the clothes and a bench for the bag. A curtain formed the door and a mosquito net hung over the bed. Some candles were lying ready for lighting. In the common rooms there were tables and chairs for meals, a few hammocks, and comfortable armchairs. A separate wooden hut housed some toilets and showers, which were fed with river water. Electricity was available in the evening from 18:00 to 22:00 from a generator, and a satellite telephone was also available in the small office. With me we were 10 guests in the camp, so it was by far not fully booked.

Every morning and afternoon there were programs with walks through the dense jungle, mostly in rubber boots, boat trips, fishing, animal watching, visiting an Indian village and many explanations about life in the jungle. During our boat trips across the river or while fishing for piranha we were often accompanied by children of the neighboring tribes in their small canoes. The boys were perhaps around six years old and steered their canoes very skillfully across the river with its eddies and small rapids. Their greatest joy was a glass of chilled lemonade from our on-board provisions. Our often-arduous hikes through the muddy and almost impenetrable jungle were mostly accompanied by mosquitoes, and occasionally our local guide had to pave our way with his machete. But we could observe many animals, spiders, various monkeys, many parrots and now and then a toucan.

My best program was the spontaneous offer of a local kitchen helper in the early morning to take me in a canoe into a small tributary at dusk. The atmosphere in the awakening forests was incredible and unique, as the canoe glided across the river with only a soft splash, the relative morning freshness in the otherwise always humid hot air, the contours of the dense green in the semi-darkness and finally the unmistakable jungle sound, right in the middle of it and undisturbed. And so many animals that one could hear but rarely see. At sunrise we were back at camp. A great experience!

Unfortunately for me the beautiful time in the camp soon came to an end, and then one morning I was sitting again in the boat that took me to Tucupita. There I should meet my driver. To my surprise it was a young woman and again I was the only passenger. During the two and a half hours of driving we had a nice conversation and I learned a lot about the life of a simple family in Venezuela. At the end I gave her the rest of my travel money in local currency, I did not need it for my already booked next-morning trip to the airport for my flight home. Her surprised and grateful look was worth it.

Chile and Brazil

My first stay in Brazil took place during the lecture tour to Arequipa, about which I have already reported. The next encounter with this country was many years later, on a trip with Cecilia, my father, and my step-mother. And this is how it came about: Through the aid organization Kindernothilfe in Duisburg, my father supported a godchild in Chile, a girl, Jimena, from a somewhat complicated patchwork family. The sponsorship made it possible for Jimena to attend a boarding school that promised school education, life assistance and vocational preparation at the same time. After many years of support and occasional correspondence, it was my father's wish to get to know Jimena personally. He had just turned 75 years old, but he did not dare to make such a journey on his own anymore, he could only imagine it with our company. So, I started to research and plan the journey. He himself clarified his plans with Jimena and the director of the boarding school by letter in his most beautiful English. Jimena did not speak English, she received appropriate translations from her boarding school, which could be understood as a benevolent censorship. When planning the trip, my stepmother's heart's desire had to be included, she wanted to see Rio de Janeiro for once in her life. Of course, this was to be respected too, although I would have preferred to plan the journey via Peru. For the extended route, I found a suitable flight with KLM, which reached Santiago de Chile with stops in Rio de Janeiro and Buenos Aires. Then the details were built in and finally a nice itinerary with a final highlight in Brazil was created.

The first leg of the journey was via Amsterdam on the long-haul flight with stopovers in Santiago de Chile. We left the hectic capital with its then about 4, today already 7 million inhabitants behind and fled with a rental car to the 110 km away Vina del Mar, the small and contemplative neighboring town of the port city Valparaiso, to recover from the effort of the long flight. The next destination was then the Hotel Termas de Jahuel, 130 km away, beautifully situated in a park at the foot of the Andes, with its own spring, which makes this oasis possible, and its own small winery. Back at Santiago International Airport we found the flight with the regional airline Ladeco to Valdivia, the hometown of Jimena, 850 km south of Santiago. There we were already welcomed at the airport by Jimena and the director of the boarding school, Sra. Campos-Reyes, as well as a student as interpreter. We were warmly welcomed and brought to the hotel in the VW bus of the boss. They had prepared a big program for the visit from Germany, but first there was a three-day round trip to the area around Lago Llanquihue, south of Valdivia.

A rental car was ready in front of the hotel at 7:00 a.m. and we started on Highway 5 south. The first destination was the big Lago Llanquihue at the edge of the Andes, directly west of the volcano Osorno, with only 2,650 m height one of the rather small volcanoes of the Chilean Andes. In this area a lot of German is spoken, and so we found smaller places with many German signs, for example cafes where on a board in front of the house "Kaffee und Kuchen" was advertised. On small roads we drove then north around the lake towards the volcano. Probably the SEAT Ibiza rented by me was actually a little too small for the four of us and the dirt road was a little too bad for his small tires, or "by chance" there was a big nail on the road, at least far away from the next village it happened then: The left rear tire was flat. I had no other choice than to take the repair into my own hands here on the spot. Luckily, the car was equipped with the necessary tools. So I managed to change the wheel under the amazed eyes of the family and - what a coincidence - in the next small town there was even a tire repair shop at the roadside, which could repair the defective tire immediately. Although we had to turn back afterwards because of the advanced time, the view of the volcano, which was snow-covered despite the low height, was impressive. We stayed overnight at the lake in the village Frutillar in the small but amazingly comfortable German speaking hotel "Klein Salzburg".

The next morning we continued northeast towards the Andes, past another lake to Lago Puyehue and then along the deep blue lake always with a view of the volcano of the same name to the Termas de Puyehue, already close to the border with Argentina. The volcano Puyehue had by the way 15 years after our visit ("one second" in the language of the volcanologists) a violent eruption, whose enormous ash cloud caused heavy damage to the agriculture in Argentina and temporarily paralyzed the air traffic in South America and hindered it up to Australia. Then it was time to return to Valdivia, where we had an appointment with Sra. Campos-Reyes for dinner in our hotel at 8:00 pm. It turned out to be a nice, relaxed, and long evening, whereby the interpreter function this time was mine. We learned a lot about the life in the poor quarter Poblacion El Laurel of the city, from which all the children of the boarding school came from, and about the necessary and useful work of the boarding school for the future of the children.

The next day was the official part of our visit to Jimena. We visited the boarding school and were happy to receive a welcome poster of Jimena. We could visit several classes and the facilities of the boarding school, the kitchen, the library, lounges and sanitary facilities, everything was exceptionally clean and tidy. The children are looked after on weekdays from 08.00 to 18.00 hours by "Tias", who look after 30 children each. For lunch there is fish and seaweed alternately, meat is too expensive. The children receive regular medical care, we were also able to visit the outpatient clinic. Then we could visit Jimena at home, in the very simple 30-year-old wooden house of her family, who lives there densely packed in a few rooms. We received a very warm welcome; it was an extremely friendly and emotional atmosphere. Jimenas mother cried at the farewell when my father gave her a guest article.
Back at the airport there was a very warm farewell from Jimena and her mother and Sra. Reyes Campos

until boarding the flight back to Santiago de Chile. With the seats on the right side we had a great final view in the evening sun to the chain of snow-covered Chilean volcanoes.

Unfortunately, this episode did not have a happy end in the end: Only a short time later Jimena disappeared from the boarding school and probably also from the city, allegedly with a man. We never heard from her again afterwards. As sad as this breakup was, maybe our support Jimena at least made her teenage years a bit more worth living.

In Santiago we had only one day available. But at least we saw the lively Plaza de Armas with the ca-thedral and its silver altar and beautiful choir stalls, which had been designed by Bavarian Jesuits. In the monastery church of San Francisco, we experienced a solemn entry of the monks. In the evening we went to the airport and with KLM via Buenos Aires to Rio de Janeiro. Actually, only to repack at the Sheraton Ho-tel, because already the next morning a new flight went via Sao Paulo to Foz do Iguacu. I did not want to miss the opportunity to present the Iguacu waterfalls to my travel company, which I still had in such a beautiful memory. But before that there was still enough time to celebrate my stepmother's birthday at her desired destination Rio de Janeiro with a glass of champagne.

And once again I was thrilled by the magnificent wa-terfalls, both from the Brazilian side and the next day from the Argentinean side - just as I was with my fellow student Elisabeth. Also, my travel companions were extremely impressed by the elemental force of the enormous water masses and the tropical vegetation around the falls with many big and beautiful butter-flies.

On the return flight to Rio de Janeiro we made a stop-over in Sao Paulo. At the Hilton Hotel we found a safe haven in the huge city, which is generally considered dangerous. Already at that time people were talking about 20 million inhabitants and a high crime rate. So, we followed the urgent recommendations of the hotel staff and limited our tours through the city to the dis-tricts that were described as reasonably safe. For din-ner I had booked a table in the restaurant at the upper floor of the Edificio Italiano that I had discovered together with Elisabeth. The Italian food was excellent and afterwards, we enjoyed on the terrace around the restaurant the unbelievable view to an unmanageable sea of skyscrapers as it was probably not available anywhere else. Above it there was a brisk air traffic from both airports of the mega city and in addition some helicopters.

And then we went back to Rio de Janeiro, but this time for real, for a few days. The Sheraton Hotel is in the south of the city, not far from the beach Ipanema. At the hotel we found a friendly and reliable driver who accompanied us on our trips into the city and who was also a valuable security consultant, because also in Rio de Janeiro the crime rate was and is high. There is a lot to see in Rio de Janeiro and our driver and companion proved to be an excellent city guide at the same time. A landmark of the city are of course the wonderful beaches, especially Ipanema and Copacabana. The Sambodromo looks empty rather plain, but one can well imagine what is going on here during the carnival. Relatively modest is the palace of the former presidents, from the time when Rio de Janeiro was the capital of Brazil. The Benedictine monastery Sao Bento from 1633 has an exceptionally beautiful monastery church with a lot of gilded wood carvings. The old cathedral was built in the style of St. Peter's in Rome with a large dome and contains many wall paintings. The new cathedral reminds in its form of the famous Mayan pyramid in Chichen-Itza in Mexico. The Carioca aqueduct, which was formerly used for water supply, is now used by trams. An absolute highlight is the ride with the cable car up to the Sugar Loaf Mountain in two stages. From the middle station, it then climbs steeply to the top of the cone. The view from there is overwhelming, a childhood dream came true for my stepmother. And an equally beautiful view can be enjoyed from the large figure of Christ above the city on Corcovado Hill.

For my father and stepmother, the stay in Rio de Janeiro was the crowning conclusion of the greatest journey of their lives. Another special experience was the final stormy landing of the KLM Boeing 747 in heavy gusts at Amsterdam Airport.

A few years later, I spontaneously had another opportunity to come to Rio de Janeiro - even over New Year's Eve. Lufthansa had - probably because of an anniversary - brought out a unique and very tempting special offer: Four days in Rio de Janeiro with a flight from Hamburg, a quite good hotel, local tour guide and a dinner together on New Year's Eve - and all that for about 1,000 €. Since I already had a frequent flyer status with Lufthansa, I found out about this offer in advance. And I managed to book eight seats for this offer. Because I had found fellow travelers very quickly: Cecilia, Abdon and his girlfriend Charlie and my good friend Arno with his three children.

So, the eight of us went to Hamburg and boarded a full Boeing 747 of Lufthansa, which took us to Rio de Janeiro. The touristic program, especially the cable car up to the Sugar Loaf Mountain, was of course like our previous trip, with the difference that this time we did not take a taxi through the city, but several coaches. The ascent to the Christ figure on the Corcovado we made this time with the rack railway, which is usually used by tourists. So was the atmosphere, a samba group entertained us already during the train ride. Abdon and me, we treated ourselves to an extra, a tandem glide from the hills down to the beach. Abdon got the kite he wanted, but for me there was only a paraglider left, but with the advantage that it could stay in the air much longer in the upwind than a kite. My flight then lasted just under half an hour. Unforgotten are also the evenings on the roof terrace of our hotel directly on the beach, where we adults took plenty of "vitamins" (Arno's name for Caipirinha) and enjoyed the evening atmosphere by the sea.

On New Year's Eve, we first went to a restaurant near the Copacabana beach to a traditional Brazilian Rodizio. In the restaurant that was occupied up to the last seat, the waiters continuously marched through the rows with oversized meat skewers and distributed the meat on the plates. In addition, there were some few side dishes and wine. Even before the best pieces of meat arrived, one was already full. In this condition, we went as a group in direction to Copacabana, where already in the early evening, there was a folk festival atmosphere. There were countless stands for bratwurst and caipirinha and with each hour, it got fuller. Finally, shortly before midnight, the people stood crowded on the beach, according to later information, approximately 2 million people were on the Copacabana. Music was everywhere and the regular supply of "vitamins" provided a good and expectant atmosphere. The absolute bang, in the true sense of the word, was then at midnight the fireworks. For more than half an hour, countless rockets and fireworks formed a huge colorful curtain in the sky above the beach and the 2 million people. Dramatic music accompanied the fireworks and every big picture was greeted with continuous cheering. It was the wonderful highlight of our spontaneous trip to Rio de Janeiro. Back to the hotel we went with our coaches, the search for a taxi would probably have been without chance. In the evening of the next day Lufthansa brought us back home again.

Chile was also recently on the program again, but only as a destination of a trip, which then led with a connecting flight to Calama and then with a rental car across the Andes to Argentina. There we went on the famous Ruta 40, the north-south connection along the eastern side of the Andes, from Salta to Mendoza, and from there again across the Andes back to Santiago de Chile. In Salta we had an appointment with Sarah, the pretty and enterprising daughter of Hartmut and Sakura, who was engaged in Argentina for a social year

in a children's home. Sarah had taken a long bus journey of over eight hours to accompany us for a day in
Salta.

Ecuador

I had already been in Ecuador for a short time from
Peru, but due to lack of time I could not get beyond
Guayaquil and Cuenca. In the meantime, I had read a
lot about this country with its many partly still active
volcanoes, the rainforest at the Rio Napo and especially the cloud forests with their diverse bird life, allegedly 2.000 species. Many years later I planned another
trip to Ecuador, which turned into three trips.

The first trip I made alone, planned were many hikes
in the cloud forests and quite simple accommodations,
so I could not convince Cecilia at first. One day after
my arrival in Quito I met my guide, Carlos, with his
pick-up truck early in the morning for the first leg of
my journey, which was to lead from Quito into the
cloud forests to the west. I was pleasantly surprised
that I was the only participant of this "small group
trip". The nature park of Yanacocha, which our first
hike led to, is just 20 km away from Quito at an altitude of a little over 3,000 m. Here at the edge of the
somewhat lower situated cloud forest region, there
were wonderful views of the volcanic mountain landscape around Quito. And there were already the first
birds to be observed, especially hummingbirds, which

are attracted to feeding places especially created for them. Similar to helicopters, hummingbirds can fly on the spot without moving around, and they use this technique especially when diving into the flowers - a nice playground for the amateur photographer to capture the birds with their lightning-fast wing movements in this position.

We continued to Mindo, 100 km away from Quito and with 1,250 m altitude in best cloud forest location, our "base camp". For the overnight stay a small circus wagon was planned for me, in which I felt quite comfortable. It even had electricity and a shower. At the common dinner in the simple restaurant we had, as on the trips, a lot of opportunity for discussion and I learned a lot about the life in Ecuador and about the current political topics of the country. Carlos was a qualified tourist guide, the studies in Ecuador include five years at a university. This way, in addition to the knowledge about the own country, a comprehensive general knowledge is also imparted.

Mindo itself is a rather touristic place and not least because of its pleasant climate a preferred and easily accessible excursion destination for the big city-plagued citizens of Quito. There are good entertainment possibilities with some attractions but also a lot of free nature in the cloud forest a little further outside. We then used both extensively. On beautiful hikes through the forests there were again many hummingbirds and even a whole family of toucans to watch and photograph. At the edge of the village we visited an orchid farm and a butterfly farm, both with beautiful specimens. Then there was also a raft ride on the river. But the highlight of the adventure program was a canopy station with ten zip-lines of different lengths over the canyons between the mountains. Already the ascent to the highest station offered beautiful views over the cloud forest. The rapid descents over the steel cables then compensated for the effort of the ascent.

Back in Quito and after an overnight stay, the second stage of the journey began, into the cloud forests located to the east, i.e. towards the Amazon region, to the San Isidro Cloud Forest Camp. In the early morning, a driver of the camp picked me up at my small hotel in Quito. After the long drive out of the city, the route continued past the Antisana volcano and over a pass about 4,000 m high up to the eastern side of the Andes chain, where the typical cloud forest regions are also halfway up. Even further down the road we went leads to the Rio Napo, which flows through the jungle further into Peru and meets the Amazon near Iquitos.

In the camp I got a comfortable wooden hut at the edge of the complex. The camp consists of the comfortably furnished common rooms and the huts scattered far over the complex as lodging for the guests. I spent my days there partly on guided hikes, partly alone birdwatching at the feeding areas, or I occasionally went out alone to explore the forest on the signposted paths. In the evening after dinner there was always a nice get-together with the other guests and the rangers with interesting and instructive discussions. The four days passed much too fast and so the driver finally brought me back to the airport of Quito.

But it should not go yet directly home, because I still had an appointment with Teresa. She had attended a training seminar for English teachers in Tacna and we had agreed to meet in Arequipa. So, I made another side trip to Peru and took an evening flight via Lima to Arequipa. We had an appointment for breakfast the next morning at 8:00 a.m., and indeed Teresa appeared, quite un-Peruvian punctual, on the beautiful balcony of the hotel with a view on the Plaza de Armas. She had also arrived late the night before by bus from Tacna. The fact that I had booked a room for her in my hotel should cause some discussions later in her family. Once again, I had underestimated the strict customs and habits in Peru.

After a long breakfast on the balcony we had a nice day together in Arequipa, the city I visited so often and where I had some nice experiences. A taxi took us to the most important sights of the city and for me to a cheap shop for my traditional alpaca shopping, as always when I was in Peru. The next morning, we took the flight to Lima together. Teresa visited her - now grown up - children there, who both had found work in Lima, Melissa as a doctor and Gianfranco in a bank. We all met again for dinner in my hotel. The next day I left Lima with KLM to return home.

The beautiful photos of the mountain landscapes, the lush forests, the birds, especially the hummingbirds and toucans, the butterflies and last but not least the orchids had convinced Cecilia quickly, so that I already planned a second trip to Ecuador together with her for the following year. This time it should also be a little more comfortable.

During my research I had discovered a luxurious boat offering 4-day trips on the Rio Napo, as well as a newly built lounge in the western cloud forest. The next trip should consist of these two components and include some more time for the capital Quito. So, for us KLM went to Quito again. The approach to the city, between the high volcanoes surrounding the city, always has a lot of turbulence and is therefore usually a bit rough. We then stayed in the city for a few days and first looked around the old town, visited the basilica and other interesting churches and let ourselves be driven up the hill Panecillo (bread roll) with the big angel figure, the Virgin of Quito, on top. The 45 meter high statue, made of 7,000 aluminum parts, was built in 1976, following the example of the much smaller "Virgen de Quito", created in 1734 by Bernardo de Legarda, which today stands on the altar in the San Francisco Monastery in Quito.

Then the journey continued by plane, from Quito in a good half hour to Coca, a small town on the Rio Napo, today - only officially - called Puerto Francisco de Orellana. The city with about 70,000 inhabitants is located at the mouth of the Rio Coca into the Rio Napo. There is also the only bridge over the Rio Napo. Today, Coca is strongly influenced by the oil industry, which unfortunately has now also penetrated this ecologically valuable area. Our idea, that our boat with the beautiful name Anaconda would have moored there, unfortunately proved to be wrong. Rather, we still had a two-hour trip in a fast, but also open feeder boat ahead of us. A beautiful ride on the river, but unfortunately the rainforest of this region lived up to its name on this day, it was raining in torrents. Thus, we arrived, despite our jackets and the provided ponchos quite drenched, finally at our boat Anaconda.

The reception was very warm. The Anaconda itself, outwardly not necessarily a beauty, but rather a rectangular box with three floors, showed then however a remarkable inner life. Luxuriously equipped cabins with full height glazed outside windows, air conditioning, a nice restaurant as well as a covered outside deck and a sun deck on the roof. A lot of staff took care of the few, altogether only eight guests. It was a comfortable place where one could really feel at home - on a river in the middle of the Amazon rainforest jungle. The days were well filled with an abundant program, with excursions into the forest in the mornings and afternoons, also at night, sometimes by walking with rubber boots, sometimes with the two small dinghies. In between there were excellent meals from rich buffets. We were enthusiastic about our scout, Freddie, who led us through the jungle and explained the flora and fauna with a lot of expertise. An Indian village was visited, but apparently also very used to the visit of the boat tourists. A daughter of the family, a pretty girl of maybe 8 years, played with a baby monkey, which she apparently kept as a pet - a feast for the photographer. Our small group also visited a school, where we also collected money for the purchase of a computer. Sensational was a sunset, which wrapped the river and the sky in a dramatic play of light and colors. At the border to Peru is the beautiful Yasuni National Park with dense, untouched jungle and many animals, which you can drive over a side arm of the Rio Napo by boat. We saw especially monkeys, iguanas, the rare pink Amazon dolphins, and we could fish for piranhas.

Back in Quito we were picked up at the hotel the next morning for our second leg of the trip. The Mashpi Lodge is very lonely, deep in the western cloud forest on the Pacific side of the Andes. From Quito we first drove a little bit towards Mindo, but soon we left the route northwards on small roads, later on narrow paths into the forest. The very luxurious lodge in generous modern construction is located at an altitude of only 950 m and offers space for 40 guests. The rooms on 5-star level with their full side windows offer a wonderful view straight into the forest. The restaurant serves fine Ecuadorian cuisine. In the mornings and afternoons, guided hikes through the forest with animal observations are offered. An observation tower for the upper levels of the cloud forest and a sky ride on a wire rope with a bicycle gondola were among the highlights of the program.

After four days of "cloud forest of the fine kind" with beautiful excursions, accompanied by small hummingbirds, big butterflies and excellent guides, we went back to Quito, and there we wanted to get to know the modern part of the city. In its center is the Plaza Foch, a popular meeting point especially for young people, surrounded by numerous good restaurants, hotels, and shops, also banks and office skyscrapers - a very lively big city experience and a nice end of the trip.

And then, again inspired by the beautiful impressions of these trips, there was a third trip to Ecuador, this time again for me alone with Abdon. I had already been with him in Peru before and had noticed that he shared my enthusiasm for the South American countries. But up to now he had not experienced the jungle in the rainforest and cloud forest yet, so I wanted to close this gap for him. In doing so I could fall back on proven destinations and so I planned our trip with another 4-day tour on the Anaconda and another stay in the cloud forest of San Isidro.

Because of cheap flights, which were only available on certain days, we started our trip with a five-day stay in Quito. A good opportunity to get to know the city and its surroundings a little bit better this time. We started with a city tour through the old as well as the modern parts of the city. We stayed near Plaza Foch, because of the good restaurants in this area. The city tour was a good idea, as the conquest of the city on foot, especially in the oldtown, can be quite exhausting due to the many ascents. And so, our bus climbed over narrow streets also the Panecillo with the big angel figure, where we enjoyed the beautiful view to the city. But there should be even more magnificent views. Because a cable car leads from the city to the Cruz Loma, after all up to a height of 4,000 m, at the east side of the volcano Pichincha. When we arrived at the upper station, the mountain was just in the clouds, but fortunately, they soon at least partly dissipated. Only from up there one recognizes how big Quito has become in the meantime, the city extends into several neighboring valleys.

Another day tour led us from Quito on the Ruta de Vulcanos about 50 km south into the region of the volcano Cotopaxi. The almost 6,000 m heighted, snow-covered but still quite active volcano last erupted in 2015, thus just between the two last mentioned trips, and it provided the capital region with a good shot of ashes. You can climb the mountain, the road leads up about 4,000 m, but for the last part of the ascent in the snow you need the appropriate equipment - and also the appropriate condition. We had decided more realistically for a smaller volcano in the same region on the other side of the Ruta de Vulcanos, the Quilotoa. Its summit, which is about 4,000 m high, can be reached on a steep mountain road. Thus, our minibus with a total of ten passengers took us there. From the edge of the volcano, one can look down to the green-blue crater lake that is approximately 300 m lower - a great view in the wild mountain landscape. A steep path leads from the edge of the crater down to the lake. For me it was enough to stand up there, but Abdon was tempted by the descent and together with some others he set off - and arrived after about 2 hours exhausted but happy back at the crater rim. In the meantime, I had spent the time and the cold with 2 or 3 Coca teas in the small restaurant at the summit with some like-minded people. The bus driver knew this procedure and had waited patiently until everybody was back.

We reached the Anaconda dry this time, but during the four-day trip the weather was much worse than I was used to last time. It rained frequently; we were in the rain forest. And this time it was astonishingly cool for the area with 25°. Especially the rainy weather in the beautiful Yasuni National Park at the border to Peru was a pity. But Abdon did not miss the opportunity to set foot on Peruvian soil at the border marker. I missed the beautiful sunsets I had enjoyed so much on my first trip on the Anaconda. Nevertheless, the experience to glide on the river through the jungle or to conquer it on our hikes on foot was again impressive and exciting. But one of the many highlights literally fell into the water: We climbed a steel scaffold about 30 m high in the pouring rain to look at the upper levels of the jungle - only to look into a wall of fog there and descend again as fast and soaked as possible. Once again the Anaconda was by far not fully booked, we were altogether only 14 guests: A Dutch family with two daughters and a son, an American couple with daughter-in-law and son, an Australian couple, a silent New Zealander and we, thus a quite international English speaking society, which had met here on the Rio Napo.

When visiting an Indian village, I had an incredibly special anaconda experience. A girl from the village reported that she had seen an anaconda in the garden of the village and was pretty excited to lead our whole group there with our guide. And indeed, there was a living anaconda in a bush, rather a younger animal of about 3 m length. Our presence and the many photos obviously annoyed her so that she left the bushes and went to another place - and this directly past my boot. The guide advised me to stand still, but I would not have thought of anything else. So, I unexpectedly got some nice photos of a veritable anaconda right in front of my foot.

Back in Quito our second leg of the journey into the cloud forest of San Isidro followed. Our driver and at the same time guide, Andres, picked us up at the airport hotel and brought us to the camp which I already knew well. Here, too, it had rained a lot during the last

110

weeks, so that in some places landslides hindered the traffic. On the way we visited a rose farm and learned that Ecuador is one of the biggest rose exporters in the world. In the meanwhile renovated and extended camp we got a nice hut and undertook with our guide Andres in the following days many excursions into the dense cloud forests. Andres was an enthusiastic bird expert, and he also succeeded in getting Abdon interested in the subject. For my part I was more interested in the forest and the lush vegetation in it. I enjoyed the few rays of sunlight that managed to get down through the dense forest to the bottom, where I could see the leaves and flowers of the variety of different plants shining like spotlights against a dark background. Whenever there was a view from a hill or in a clearing, one could see shreds of clouds wafting through the forest or occasionally looking at a thick wall of fog, in front of which the trees appeared like shadows in the haze. Again and again, a light drizzle showed that one was between clouds.

As a further highlight I had booked the "Amazon Dinner" for one evening, a compilation of culinary specialties from the Amazon region in several courses, unusual but delicious. Only the last course I had to enjoy alone, because an owl had just been spotted in the camp...

Due to increasing landslides and the resulting road closures, Andres urgently recommended us to leave one day in advance in order not to miss our flight due to unplanned stops. So we did, and for the next night Andres was able to put us up in another camp in similar surroundings but closer to the airport. The particularly critical part of the road was already behind us with some small delays - a reassuring feeling. The

Guango-Lodge has only a few rooms and a comfortable dining room, which was heated with a smoking wood stove during the cool rainy weather. Our room was tiny, but for one night it was completely sufficient. The next day we arrived punctually at the airport of Quito.

And then we went to Peru for a short time. I wanted to show Abdon more of Lima, which was a bit too short on the last trip. Unfortunately, Teresa was on vacation in the USA with her family at that time, so we could not meet each other. So, I had to give the travel guide alone. For that, I got professional help.

We stayed in my home base, the Fourpoints Hotel in Miraflores. The next morning, we met our guide, a charming young woman, for an exclusive half-day city tour that took us not only to the famous sights but also to places in the city I had never seen before. For the evening I had booked an incredibly special highlight far in advance, a dinner at Astrid & Gaston, one of the best restaurants in Lima. Lima has long been considered a stronghold of fine Peruvian cuisine, and Gaston, head of this restaurant and a cooking school, was one of its most prominent representatives. We were not disappointed; it was simply terrific! Under the name "lima love" Gaston presented a tasting menu in twelve courses and with a matching wine accompaniment, a culinary delight! But the contrast to the full-day program of the next day could not be greater!

The Lima Local Communities Tour took us both with two guides to the poor outlying areas in the south of the city. The tour started quite contemplative with a visit to the local fish market at the Playa Pescadores in the district Barranco. We looked at the variety of fish-es and afterwards we went out to sea on a fishing boat to enjoy the panorama of the city from there. Many boats were on the way and repeatedly landed new fish. Then we continued in a long drive through the almost endless and densely populated district of San Juan de Miraflores up to the edge of the city, which borders on the mountains of the Andes in a hilly landscape. In this hilly landscape, the poor districts of the city are located, roughly speaking the further up the hills the poorer. The electricity and water supply only reach up to about half of the height, the simple houses and huts above are supplied with water by tank trucks. In this area we got the opportunity to meet some people who live there. We talked to a woman who had come with her family from the mountains to the city through sheer misery and was now trying to make a living with partly bought and partly self-produced handicraft articles. This was not a good business prospect in the simple hut at the upper edge of the settlement, far away from all streams of tourists. The yield was prob-ably only enough for the most basic needs. So, it was of course also in the sense of our tour, which is rather rarely carried out, to provide some additional turnover here.

In another settlement, also above the electricity and water border, we met a woman who organizes a facili-ty for childcare, games and homework help are of-fered there. This is not a governmental institution; it was only created by self-help of the inhabitants of this settlement. For this purpose, they had built a simple house and also the care of the children was organized by themselves. It touched me when we learned that some children have to freeze in cold weather - and even more so when I spontaneously offered the woman my old Peruvian alpaca jacket for such a child and she thanked me very much. A donation for the children's house also changed hands, as a toilet was still missing.

We met another woman who had organized a common kitchen for a larger circle, in which the food purchased was shared. We were impressed by the willingness to help themselves and the sense of community of the extremely poor inhabitants of this settlement, who organize their lives together practically without any help from the state. Finally, we were invited to eat in one of the huts, there was delicious rice with beans. We cooked on a wood stove and the water came from the tanker.

This stark contrast between the opulent and extremely luxurious dinner in the restaurant of Astrid y Gaston and the simple but very cordial hospitality in this hut kept us very busy during the return trip and also during the flight back to Germany the next day. Abdon, too, gained important impressions of living together in other countries and cultures during his two trips to Peru and Ecuador.

Reflections about travelling

Travel gives experience

Traveling is perhaps the most important, but in any case, the most beautiful way to gain life experience. This is also expressed by the Brazilian writer Paolo Coelho:

"Las grandes lecciones que aprendi fueron precisamente aquellas que los viajes me ensenaron."
(The great lessons I learned were those that travel taught me)

I would sign this immediately. Because travelling (not necessarily the beach holiday) has a much greater potential to see, experience and learn new things than the normal everyday life. If you can open up to the new with all your senses and bring along a portion of curiosity and empathy, then the channel for the reception of life experience is wide open.

In this narrative I have limited myself to journeys to South America. I could also write other stories about travel experiences in North America or those from the quite different islands of the Caribbean. But South America, and Peru in particular, have always been special destinations for me, and I have developed a very personal and deeply felt relationship to this region with its people, its landscapes and its music. You can also love a country.

The journeys described here took place over a period of a good 4 decades. And so they are journeys as they could hardly be more different: Travelling with an old cloak-and-cloth bag and those with a suitcase, travelling with a good travel budget and those with the smallest budget, travelling in business class and those in low-cost airlines with endless stopovers, travelling with a map and compass and those with a smartphone - and finally travelling in a group, travelling in pairs and travelling alone.

Travelling alone

Travelling alone is a special challenge, but at the same time an important experience. With a travel partner it is much easier, four eyes see more than two. When you go to the toilet, this becomes immediately clear: your partner will look after your luggage during the time you are absent. Leaving luggage unattended when travelling alone is not a good idea in most countries, not only in South America. So there are two possibilities to take your luggage to the toilet, which you usually can't and don't really want to do, or you can look around and ask someone in the neighborhood to look after your luggage for a few minutes. A first good exercise in communication with the locals! Because even outside of this special situation, with only two eyes and two arms, you will be dependent on help from strangers from time to time.

In contrast to a trip as a couple or even an organized group trip, as a single traveler you are, so to speak, an entrepreneur in your own business and have to take care of everything and anything yourself at all times: Travel and day planning, transport connections and timetables, luggage transport, accommodation, finances, your own safety and finally entertainment. A certain amount of management skills and self-confidence is required. Time and again, situations, encounters, weather conditions or breakdowns occur that require replanning or improvisation. The bus does not arrive, the car gets stuck, a thunderstorm is coming, all accommodations are fully booked, a pickpocket tries his luck - there are so many reasons why a day does not go exactly as planned! In the age of package tours with a fully comprehensive insurance and return guarantee, it has perhaps become somewhat out of focus that travelling to other countries and other continents always involves risks: illness, injuries, crime, forces of nature and failures of the infrastructure lurk everywhere. An old Persian proverb from pre-Islamic times says

"The best thing you get from traveling home is uninjured skin."

But then it is much more than that! The reward for the effort is more than worth every effort: an incredible feeling of freedom, which you can experience just as little in the usually well-worn everyday life at home as on thoroughly organized package tours. And in addition, a great satisfaction when you have once again managed a self-planned and organized day's stage in the evening, or simply marched off "into the blue" and arrived somewhere. That is how aptly the Spanish singer and songwriter Joan Manuel Serrat describes this feeling of freedom of the unaccompanied traveler with his wonderful lines in his song "Cantares":

"Caminante, son tus huellas el camino y nada mas,
Caminante, no hay camino, se hace camino al andar."
(Wanderer, your tracks are the path and nothing more,
Wanderer, there is no path, the path is made by walking)

Luggage is an important and in the truest sense of the word a serious and sensitive issue, after all you must carry it all by yourself! And luggage is extremely attractive for some specialized professions, and it is also quite vulnerable to attacks. That is why I am not a big fan of the backpack, which likes to be attacked from behind in the crowd. Probably the most impractical piece of luggage is the trolley bag if you are not in airports and on polished surfaces. When travelling alone, I usually prefer the shoulder bag, which you can carry in the front, back or side or hold in your hand. But probably the most important solution for luggage of the person travelling alone is: as little and as light as possible! If only because of the "sensitivity".

And then there is the loneliness. You should know what to do with yourself, read, write, sort your thoughts when it gets lonely, or dream - but only with one eye on your luggage. And soon you miss company, the exchange of thoughts, the touch, you get jealous when you meet a couple. Like at a station of the Peruvian railway between Cusco and Juliaca, where I looked out of the window and could watch how two Australian boys bid a very heartfelt farewell to two girls they had apparently met there a few days or maybe the evening before. A sight that makes you feel like you are missing something. And sometimes one also asks oneself: What am I doing here all alone? But - and this is the other side - at the same time one becomes more open to take in impressions, to look at the surroundings and for contact and communication with strangers. I have met many people on my journeys alone and have made several good friends, both locals and travelers from various other countries. Impressions you gather on the way and contacts are usually more intensive than when you travel in a group and are more occupied with each other. This makes travelling alone especially valuable for your own personality and life experience. In any case, I have always found travelling and especially travelling alone to be a great enrichment of my life.

Technology and money

Travelling without a smartphone is probably unimaginable for the younger generations today. Without being reachable at all times, without always being able to call for help, without today's navigation aids, maps and route planning, without the bus timetable or flight schedule at the touch of a button and without the possibilities of entertainment or communication when it gets lonely, is that even possible? The answer is yes, it works! Most of my travels through South and Central America have never had a smartphone. That is why I did not have the opportunity to see this as a disadvantage. Route planning and navigation indeed work with good maps and a compass. You can also ask for flight and timetables, good travel guides with lots of useful detailed information are also available as a book. Most of the time I travelled with the very compact and small printed South American Handbook, the bible of all South American travelers at that time. Instead of entertainment from the smartphone, there was the preparation of the next stages with the handbook.

And today probably quite unimaginable: I received messages from family or friends mostly poste restante at the main post office in Lima. This was cumbersome for both parties, and my mail was therefore always rather limited. But Lima is a little bit like Paris: Since there are almost no connections between other cities within Peru, the journey was always via the capital and so I had the opportunity to stop by the post office. From the post office it was of course also possible to make phone calls, but they were so incredibly expensive that I hardly ever used them.

Surely the Smartphone offers considerable facilitations when travelling and a large measure of additional security. Nobody today will want to do without it without need. The demands on the "entrepreneur" travelling alone are becoming less stringent. However, a good piece of adventure is also lost in the process. But even with a smartphone you are well advised not only to rely on it, because by no means everywhere in South America a compatible network is available to the tourist. And maybe even if you urgently need the little helper in a lonely area, there is a radio blackout "on duty".

Let us still talk about money. It is particularly useful, but travelling is also possible without much money. There is a broad market of travel possibilities, for very small, small, large and very large budgets. I have practiced various things over the years, and I cannot say that the lowest-budget trips were less interesting and eventful than the luxury trips. That starts with the flight. Of course, it is very pleasant and comfortable to travel in business class, but the much cheaper economy class also gets you to your destination. For both, with meticulous searches and a little flexibility in the question of dates, you can usually find particularly favorable offers, numerous platforms on the net are specialized in finding such offers. The cheapest prices are often associated with longer or unfavorable flight times, but that's just the way it is. And also, with regard to transport connections and accommodation in the destination country, there is an equally wide range of prices in all conceivable comfort classes. In fact, it is still possible to travel through South America with little money. Simple life is not expensive there, the wages in South America are much lower.

The search for happiness

The search for happiness is inherent in man, probably everyone does it - and everyone in his own unique way. The possibilities of finding happiness are also not the same for all people, if only because material goods are distributed very differently. There are huge differences in the distribution of material goods between rich and poor countries, as well as between rich and poor people in these countries. Without wanting to come into the suspicion of unreflective egalitarianism, I consider these differences to be much too great for my own personal feeling. Nevertheless, during my travels I have also made the experience that material endowment has little to do with happiness. In our culture we are strongly influenced by the desire to achieve and increase prosperity, and for many people it is a great feeling of happiness to be able to buy a new and bigger or better car. Even more surprising when you travel to areas where such a thing would not be financially feasible, and people are still just as happy - or even more? Because the pursuit of ever greater prosperity also generates stress and unhappiness. Again and again, when I travelled to areas that one would call poor from a local perspective, I was impressed by how happy and self-evident people there are with their lives and their life situation. It is obviously other, non-material values and experiences that create happiness there. They are also often better at celebrating than we are. And nobody there must worry about crashing investments. Such experiences have always made me very thoughtful. Everyone may become happy according to his own way, but for me personally, such experiences have changed - or rather expanded - my understanding of happiness.

"We have learned that happiness lies in profundity and grows in silence",
I wrote this in the advertisement for my wedding with Cecilia in 1990; it referred to a harmonious relation-

ship between two people, perhaps the greatest possible potential for happiness. But isn't it also happiness to make a job a success, for example to finish a book, win a prize, win the lottery - or buy a new car? Happiness is so versatile, individual, and relative. And it is also fleeting, you must work on it again and again. Even the lottery million would otherwise only be temporary, the new car would soon be an old model again. The "happiness that lies in profundity", on the other hand, seems to be perhaps more enduring? But you must work on it again and again.

Does travel make you happy? I mean yes. The small and big challenges that one successfully overcomes, experiencing magnificent landscapes, experiencing support, hospitality and mutual sympathy, immersion in foreign values and customs, in foreign music and in another language. All this contains a lot of potential for happiness, the more active and open-minded a journey is designed and experienced.

And finally, one's own growth in life experience is also connected with happiness. Life experience gives security, sovereignty and maybe even a piece of wisdom. The experiences from abroad leave you a bit above the limited everyday view and thus convey more serenity, a privilege that makes life easier and more pleasant - and happier? This makes it even more important to me to enable young people to have these experiences and thus this privilege and happiness. The children of my friends and acquaintances, who were given the chance to spend a few months or a year abroad, all came back home significantly enriched by important life experiences. There are many offers for this, also with state support, you just have to make an effort.

Traveling is time-consuming, can be expensive and is often exhausting. For some of the journeys described here, I have had to endure considerable hardships. And mostly I did it with pleasure, I learned quickly how much it is worth it.

Climate and Corona

I am writing this text almost two years after the worldwide movement for the climate "Fridays for Future" (FFF) came into being and a few months after the start of the likewise worldwide corona pandemic in 2020. At the moment, traveling as described here is hardly possible. Many countries have imposed entry bans or only allow entry with a quarantine obligation of several weeks. Even postal traffic is no longer possible to many countries. The sky is empty, civil air traffic has come to a virtual standstill, and the large airfields in Germany have mutated into aircraft parking lots. I could not have imagined beforehand that all air traffic could almost come to a standstill so quickly, almost worldwide. Even at Düsseldorf airport, near where I live, it has become incredibly quiet. Almost only small private planes take off and land, and occasionally cargo flights as well. The aircraft noise here near the airport, which as a frequent flyer I always liked to call the "Sound of Freedom", has disappeared, the singing of the birds in the garden now seems much louder than before. Nobody knows, when there will be air traffic like last year and if there will it be again. Some airlines are already bankrupt and have filed for bankruptcy, others are about to do so. Some airlines, for example Lufthansa, Air France and KLM, receive large sums of money as support from the state. Flying is just, on the routes where it is still possible at all, amazingly cheap, there are some incredible special offers, probably out of desperation to be able to occupy at least some planes at all. However, probably with the resumption of flight operations, due to the reduced capacities caused by bankruptcies, prices are likely to rise again significantly. But the Corona pandemic is not the only problem for aviation.

Flying is also an emotionally charged topic in the current climate debate. The FFF founder Greta Thunberg has publicly declared, among other things, that she will not be taking any air travel at all as her personal contribution to climate protection. Flight shaming was born. If this were to become a model, trips to other continents would no longer be possible. Because not everyone, like Greta Thunberg, is provided with a fast and seaworthy sailing yacht for a lecture trip to the USA and has two weeks time for the crossing. However, the fact that many journalists travelled by plane to the starting point and destination of this trip cast doubt on the sense of this PR campaign. The crew of the boat, which was replaced at the destination, also took the plane for the return trip, as did the new crew for the journey.

I do not want to be misunderstood: Climate protection is an urgent necessity and will not tolerate any further delay! And Greta Thunberg's commitment to this is honorable and admirable. Climate protection needs radical demands now, but the side effects must also be kept in mind and weighed up. The corona pandemic has now given the climate an unexpected respite: not only has passenger air traffic been massively reduced worldwide, by over 90 percent in Germany alone, but industry has also been cut back considerably, and private road traffic has also fallen sharply at times. This shows what is basically possible - but also with considerable side effects. Previously strong companies (automotive, aviation, tourism) are experiencing massive slumps, some are on the verge of bankruptcy after only a few months of "shutdown". Unemployment is rising dramatically, and some sectors with many small businesses (catering, events, culture) are threatened with the loss of numerous livelihoods.

Apart from these massive damages, the loss of the possibility to travel is also close to my heart. This is immaterial damage, but no less significant because of it. I had already explained why I consider travel - also and especially to other continents - to be so important, especially for young people. The importance of these experiences for one's own personality, but also for living together in our society, can hardly be overestimated. Whether a frequent flier existence, as I have lived it, is still appropriate in the future seems very questionable to me. One could have made many concessions and will probably have to do so in the future. Short-haul flights, low-cost flights and certainly also some business trips could have been avoided anyway - for the sake of the climate this would be a big and good step. This also applies to other types of travel. In this context, for example, the popular but very polluting cruise shipping should also be reconsidered. In principle, however, travel should remain possible and affordable.

The most important question now seems to me to be whether we will succeed in finding a new start out of the Corona crisis, one that integrates the requirements of climate protection into the reviving economic situation. Individual approaches are already apparent, the bicycle is booming, the video conferences and home office required in the shutdown have proved their worth overall and could make countless business trips and commuting unnecessary in the future. But it is bottom-up solutions that have developed. A more far-reaching top-down strategy on the part of politicians, on the other hand, is hardly discernible at present. Although politicians in Germany have so far been quite successful in managing the corona crisis to begin with, the strategy has already torn itself apart into numerous regional autonomies, disputes, and vanities. The next election sends its regards.

In addition, a climate catastrophe can probably only be prevented by joint international efforts. One million electric cars in Germany, possibly fed by coal-fired power stations, do not yet do any climate protection - and even that would be a political feat. A promising climate-friendly alternative, hydrogen technology, could only be realized if international agreements could guarantee the safety of hydrogen production from solar energy in sunny countries and of the transport routes. Stopping the deforestation of the rainforests, perhaps the most important task for climate protection of all, would probably only be achievable through massive international pressure, which requires unity. Is today's world already ready for this? Or does the predicted catastrophe first have to become evident? Then it could be too late. If, for example, the permafrost continues to thaw, the catastrophe will probably be unstoppable. Even if I found the sailboat trip to New York silly and unnecessary - Greta is right, it is high time for a "Bazooka against climate change"!

Friendship

On my trips to South America I met many people and made many friends. This is an aspect of travel that has always been particularly important to me, but whose actual value I now appreciate even more and more. There were fleeting acquaintances, many more than are explicitly mentioned in this story. There were also friendships that did not withstand the distance and the spatial separation for a long time, and which were not forgotten but did not live on actively. And there remained friendships that began on the journeys and that still belong to my valuable and active circle of friends today: Jostein and Randi from Norway, whose traditional annual meeting with Cecilia and me is regularly a highlight of the year, also Jörg from Switzerland, now with his wife Renate, as well as Hartmut from Hamburg, now with his wife Sakura, are also always welcome guests in our house. Also, the connection to

Martha and Winfried lasted for a long time. Many other friendships and acquaintances, such as Maria and Grace in Arequipa or Consuelo in Trujillo and some others have accompanied and enriched my travels, even if they did not last forever.

And then there is Teresa, my friend from Chiclayo, who I already met on my first trip to South America in the train to Machu Picchu. Often, we met again in Peru afterwards, twice she has already visited us in Düsseldorf. The magic of Machu Picchu at our first meeting touched us, the prophecy was fulfilled and a wonderful and probably - as promised - lifelong friendship was born. The myth of Machu Picchu is still alive.